Seven Steps to
Transform Your
Church

Other Books by Bill Hull

Jesus Christ, Disciple Maker
The Disciple-Making Pastor
The Disciple-Making Church
Building High Commitment in a Low-Commitment World

Seven Steps to
Transform
Your
Church

Bill Hull

Fleming H. Revell
A Division of Baker Book House Co
Grand Rapids, Michigan 49516

© 1993 by Bill Hull

Published by Fleming H. Revell
a division of Baker Book House Company
P.O. Box 6287, Grand Rapids, MI 49516-6287

Paperback edition published 1997

Previously published under the title *Can We Save the Evangelical Church?*

Printed in the United States of America

Library of Congress Cataloging-in-Publication Data

Hull, Bill, 1946–
    Seven steps to transform your church / Bill Hull.—Pbk. ed.
      p. cm.
    Includes bibliographical references.
    ISBN 0-8007-5615-0 (paper)
    1. Church renewal. 2. Evangelistic work. 3. Evangelism. I. Title.
BV600.2.H546 1997
262'.001'7—dc21   96-48114

Contents

Introduction

I believe the evangelical church can be saved. In fact, I believe it can be restored to relevancy as well as holiness, and it can reap a great harvest. In order for this to happen, however, evangelical Christians must change. We must change our ways, and we must change the perception of our mission.

Today, the evangelical church exists to serve the evangelical Christian. But if our mission is to reach the world, we must begin to think about the unchurched, those outside Christ. We must focus on those who have not yet found their needs met in what the church has to offer. The only way to save evangelicalism from the junkyard of irrelevancy is to put mission first and ourselves second. When this happens, the needs of both the unreached and the evangelical will be met. I believe it can happen, but first a confession.

The evangelical church leaves a bad taste in my mouth. Oh, I know I am a disciple of my culture with an imperfect perception and prejudiced views. I love the church. I have given myself to it. I have dedicated my life to returning it to its disciplemaking roots. But, I agree with Howard Snyder, "It is hard to escape the conclusion that today one of the greatest roadblocks to the gospel of Jesus Christ is the institutional church."[1]

The present condition of the evangelical church is appalling in light of our purpose. Bonhoeffer said, "The Church is the Church only when it exists for others."[2] If the purpose of the church is to glorify God by making disciples of all nations, then we are failing. The average evangelical church in North America exists for itself. Churches are preoccupied with themselves, their routines, locations, facilities, and filling up their buildings for performances. Although you can find pockets of effectiveness, most of evangelicalism is too self-centered to change its structures and move out of its comfort zone.

In today's church, one hundred adults and one year are required to introduce 1.7 people to Christ.[3] The alarming fact is that 50 percent of evangelical churches do less than that. Most churches could do a better job of reaching those in need of Christ if they would close down the church and hire one person to go door-to-door. In ten hours a week, such a person could reap a greater harvest than do many of our churches. About 80 percent of American churches have either plateaued or are in decline. Many stall out because, as insulated islands of Christians, they do not even try to relate to the unchurched in their communities. This might sound too harsh, but the facts substantiate the judgment.

The problem of the evangelical church is multidimensional. Many churches are trapped in a bureaucratic morass. Our best people are involved in keeping the machinery moving, rather than out on the front lines where they belong. We spend most of our money on ourselves, making sure we are full-service, Christian outlets. Our pastors are frustrated, our lay people burned out, and our programs superficial.

Most of my waking hours are filled with traveling and teaching church leaders. I repeat here what I hear over and over again. The recurring themes declare a serious indictment against the way we are "doing church." We spend billions of dollars, but most of it might as well be washed down the drain.

The Lion Has Roared

An eerie parallel can be drawn between the contemporary church and the Old Testament nation of Israel. When the kingdom divided, a displeased God appointed a prophet to declare his message. Amos became the reluctant prophet to the northern ten tribes of Israel. This simple sheep herder was given the task of pronouncing judgment whenever he went to market.

The prophet's words stung Israel's pride, and the people complained that this "hick" was upsetting everyone. If the country could have secured a restraining order, it most certainly would have done so. Amos did not want to cause trouble or make enemies or alienate his friends, but God had spoken. "The lion has roared—who will not fear? The Sovereign LORD has spoken—who can but prophesy?" (Amos 3:8). Israel's sin was as serious then as the evangelical church's sin now. The prophet painted a picture of inner decay. In Israel, judges were taking bribes; immorality was the rule. Amos spoke about the difference between belief and practice, and he preached against social injustice. Crushing the poor was sin. The people in Israel may have responded to Amos' breast-beating by asking him what he was talking about. Prophets are such pessimists and sanctimonious fussbudgets! Look at our wonderful churches. They are filled, they are growing. This is a time of great harvest. The country stood by as God passed judgment on seven neighbors: Damascus, Gaza, Tyre, Edom, Ammon, Moab, and Judah. In a move that surprised Israel, God pronounced his judgment against them, too.

Church watcher George Barna writes, "A recent national survey discovered that no fewer than seven out of ten Christians are prone to hedonistic attitudes about life."[4] The study found strong support among Christians for the 1960s' notion that an individual is free to do whatever pleases him, as long as it does not hurt others. Two out of five Christians believed such thinking is proper, thus effectively rejecting the unconditional code of ethics and morality taught in the Bible. A similar proportion of born-again people denied the possibility that pain or suffering can bring maturity. This, of course, refutes the scriptural teaching that pain and suffering can be a means to perfect our faith. Three out of ten Christians agreed that "nothing in life is more important than having fun and being happy."[5]

The contemporary church has recently witnessed the demise of many orthodox friends. The past thirty years have brought a serious decline in mainline denominations. From 1965 to 1985, liberal denominations have suffered heavy losses: Presbyterian—24 percent; Episcopal—20 percent; United Methodist—16 percent; and the Disciples of Christ—42 percent. At the same time, some denominations have grown: Assemblies of God—116 percent; Church of God—147 percent; Church of the Nazarene—50 percent; and Southern Baptist—34 percent.[6]

A superficial analysis yields the quick conclusion that liberals are in serious trouble while the evangelicals are reaping a great harvest; therefore, the evangelical church is not in trouble. But the fact remains that, since the 1940s, the evangelical church has not grown in proportion to population growth.[7] Evangelical churches have grown in terms of absolute members, but as a percentage of total population, they have declined. Many churches have grown because of demographic changes, not because of evangelism. We have watched God remove his hand from the major denominations. We have thought, *It's too bad, but they deserve it.* We think ourselves safe from God's discipline because we are theologically orthodox and we are the church, not Israel. We reason that this is God's age of grace. He doesn't hammer his people anymore. However, I firmly believe the Lion has roared against the evangelical church.

What is the sin of the evangelical church? We have lost our heart for the world. We are like Laodicea—tepid. We do not care enough about our ways to fulfill our mission. **In functional terms, the church has not obeyed the Lord's commission to make disciples. Because of this disobedience, it is suffering.** When the church makes disciples, it gets healthy Christians who can reproduce. This provides it with willing workers who are less likely to burn out and whose gifts do not exceed their character. Additionally, it is also blessed with effective leaders who are the key to long-term expansion.

The body is not healthy. An unhealthy body is not able to carry on strong evangelism. Our churches are populated with members who are not ready to evangelize others. Many pastors have failed to equip their members to carry out the task. This great failure has created a church of weakness, dominated by a "what about me?" mentality.

Many well-intentioned church leaders would like to break out of this prison of structures and bureaucratic red tape, but entrenched controllers will not let them. We have a two-edged sword, one edge represented by those who live in the spirit of James and John who said in a solemn moment to Christ, "Give us what we want" (Mark 10:35). They are superficial consumers who love affluence and themselves too much to break patterns and reach the lost. The other edge is represented by "hard core" traditionalists who love their church too much to break away from mere structures and reach the lost. This is a grievous sin, and we must repent now.

We Need Renewal

The evangelical church desperately needs a fresh touch from God, yet not everyone believes it is worth the trouble. Some are now telling us to leave the institutional church behind and plant new churches. Dr. Ralph Neighbor writes, "After devoting nearly a quarter of a century to the attempt to help renew the churches, I am a total skeptic that it can be done."[8] Neighbor loves the church and has given himself fully to its mission, but I disagree with his conclusion. I prefer to cast my lot with Elton Trueblood who wrote, "The Church or something like it must be cherished, criticized, nourished, and reformed."[9] The question, "Can we save the evangelical church?" originated with church leaders. I have lost count of how many times a dedicated pastor or church leader has asked me this question. These are not skeptics; they are committed workers who have said yes to the Great Commission. They have said yes to reaching the unreached and building the Church of Jesus Christ. But they have found that the traditional church is talking out of both sides of its mouth, giving a hearty "amen" to the Great Commission and an entrenched "no" to the change required.

No wonder leaders are now asking if there is any hope for the church. The answer is not a simple one. But I believe it can be done, if we commit ourselves to a set of convictions and strategies. That is what this book is all about.

Part 1

We Must Heed the Lion's Roar

or

First Things First

1

Renewal

B efore anything else, church renewal is a matter of the heart. It is gut-wrenching prayer, Spirit-generated confession, determined repentance, and conflict resolution. It is the work of the Holy Spirit. It is those internal spiritual issues that must not be skipped. If they are, then moving on to secondary renewal issues, such as mission statements, restructuring, or evangelism strategy, will be pointless. We must not be too interested in superficial changes that only relieve symptoms and bring temporary relief—a plop, plop, fizz, fizz theology.

There are so many statements today about renewal and revival. Some write books and preach about revival or renewal without ever having experienced it. Many wait for a special visitation from God. This is Christianity in the passive voice. Christianity is experienced more in the middle voice, that is, God and believer sharing responsibility.

The elements for renewal are available to the church today. Charles Finney believed renewal was possible whenever it was desired. The Puritans prescribed a certain method, believing that revival would spring from the faithful completion of normal disciplines. But renewal is neither mechanical nor totally out of our control. Rather, it is a matter of grasping hold of what has already been given.

Is it possible that the means God employed in earlier days to renew his church were different than the methods he plans to utilize now? In the past God used long revival meetings. But this model depends on getting people to a certain location for an extended period of time to attend an event. In today's changing culture, few people will attend such meetings. Renewal today must, of necessity, be more process than event. The methods of reaching people now must change. Instead of the failed policy of motivating non-Christians to attend church, the church must go to the people. In fact, this concept is the primary biblical model. The proper flow is Christians going to church and then going to the world. There are too many attempting to reverse the flow. The philosophy of some is build it and they will come or entertain them and they will come. This is only partially true and this philosophy is unsatisfactory with respect to reaching the world for Jesus Christ. Because so few will be reached by that methodology, God's secret plan for reaching the world is for his disciples to multiply over and over and over. The reason why the world is not presently evangelized is our disobedience—our refusal to take seriously his command to make disciples.

What needs to happen before true renewal can take place? Church leaders everywhere are asking this question. Clearly, the church must want it. However, before it can happen, church members must be convinced it is needed.

The majority of Americans consider the church irrelevant.[1] The traditional church consists of a building, a pastor, and a flock. However, this model is not working! A study by the Home Missions Board of the Southern Baptist Convention shows that 33 percent of our churches plateau at 50 members, 33 percent at 150 members, 28 percent at 350 members, and only 5 percent at more than 1,000 members.[2] George Gallup's research indicates that only 12 percent of Americans are committed Christians. A large group, 28 percent, go to church but are not committed. Another 45 percent do not attend church but are receptive. New agers, atheists, and others comprise the remaining 15 percent.[3]

Bob Gilliam, one of the country's foremost church consultants, deduces that it takes the average evangelical church one year and one hundred members to introduce one person to Christ.[4] To make matters worse, many such churches are wasting people's lives, driving pastors out of the ministry, and turning away those seeking God.

Many churches in deep trouble today do not know it, or know it but are ignoring it. All of the statistics in the world will not bring about change anymore than knowing that 40 percent of Americans are overweight will motivate a person to diet. Looking in a mirror and being put off by what one sees will motivate someone to diet. By looking at ourselves and recognizing what needs to be changed, we will begin to take the necessary steps toward renewal. It's like the frog in the kettle. The temperature is rising. Will he jump out? What will get us to jump out of the kettle?

Church historian Richard Lovelace presents a model for contemporary church renewal. Lovelace says the preconditions for renewal must be addressed. These two preconditions are awareness of God's holiness and awareness of the depth of man's sin.[5] In the "great missionary explosion of the Second Evangelical Awakening, information and prayer were the catalysts for action,"[6] Lovelace writes. I would put it in slightly different terms. For a church to change, it must first experience insight, then pray a prayer of repentance, and finally a prayer of inquiry concerning God's plan for it.

Quite often, we desire change to meet ego needs, i.e. the need to be noticed, to feel good about ourselves and our work. In fact, many of us meet these needs by pursuing them under the sanctified banner of the gospel. Evangelical leaders are no exception. It is frightening how often trends are taught as biblical absolutes. Pastors flock to seminars for the latest and hottest trends that will cause their churches to grow. It becomes addictive—going from conference to conference, from megachurch to megachurch. It breeds a generation of methodological junkies.

I have attended many seminars in search of that right method or technique to make my church grow. I admit I often wanted the method to bring growth because growth made me feel good about myself. Some leaders are even willing to change theological conviction in order to experience growth. Many pastors, once critical of the "third wave" or "signs and wonders" movement, are now advocates. One wonders if, when they had their hands in the air, their egos didn't pick their theological pockets. Did God convince them that their theology was wrong or was their change facilitated by the meeting of their own ego needs? Pastors and church leaders must explore this issue for their local churches before their churches can move toward renewal.

Asking God to renew a church is risky business. Navigating through the terrain of lust, ego, and ungodly goals is treacherous. Our present cultural mood contributes to the difficulty of sorting out motive. While

I believe that, this side of heaven, we cannot perfectly decipher motive, a church must seek God and ask him to reveal the authenticity of motive. He is equipped for such a task and has told us he will handle it (1 Cor. 3:10–16). Frustration with difficulty is not sufficient motive for renewal. Most often, our reason for seeking help is to correct the bad and replace it with the good. A church needs more motive behind its actions than the fact that attendance and giving are down, or crisis and expenses are up. The leaders must seek a higher motive. Otherwise, we look like poor leaders and get criticized when things do not improve.

Paul stated it well, "In order that we, who were the first to hope in Christ, might be for the praise of his glory" (Eph. 1:12). "His intent was that now, through the church, the manifold wisdom of God should be made known to the rulers and authorities in the heavenly realms, according to his eternal purpose which he accomplished in Christ Jesus our Lord" (Eph. 3:10–11). This is the right motivational purpose for contemporary man. For true renewal to take place, we must get to the point of giving God glory. This must be our true motivation.

God has thankfully provided us with a practical handle for reaching this highest motivation—**obedience to the commanded mission of the church.** John 15:8 fits perfectly with Christ's command in Matthew 28:19 to "make disciples of all nations." It tells us that "this is to my Father's glory, that you bear much fruit, showing yourselves to be my disciples." A church must give itself to the mission Christ commanded. However, growth cannot be the motive; neither can needs nor offerings nor the youth ministry. The motive must be a desire to please God by bearing fruit and reaching others for Christ. Christ came to seek and save that which is lost. If we, as his church, do the same, we will move more deeply into knowing and loving him. As we build our relationship with God, the developing intimacy with him will form the basis for the right motive. Our daily obedience to Christ will flow from our desire to please him and give him glory. Once church leaders question their motive for renewal and seek the right motive, they will be prepared to move forward toward the next step which is prayer.

2

Prayer and Repentance

The Acts of the Apostles demonstrates a clear connection between dependent prayer and effective mission. In chapters 1, 4, 12, and 13, expansion of mission is followed by focused corporate prayer. "Lord, teach us to pray," the disciples requested in Luke 11:1. The Lord then instructed them in the Lord's Prayer. In *With Christ in the School of Prayer*, Andrew Murray provides a simple map to assist seekers in their quest to walk with God. "First, thy name, thy kingdom, thy will; then, give us, forgive us, lead us, deliver us. The lesson is of more importance than we think. In true worship the Father must be first, must be all. The sooner I learn to forget myself in the desire he may be glorified, the richer will the blessing be that prayer will bring to myself. No one ever loses by what he sacrifices for the Father."[7] Scripture teaches that seeking God first is a commanded objective (Matt. 6:33). The pursuit of God for God himself is the most pristine of all motives. And such pursuit requires prayer.

Many of us know very little about heartfelt seeking after God (Jer. 29:13). It would be a new experience for many. Church leaders must call the church to prayer in order to teach members how to pray and seek God. Modeling and doing are, by far, the best teachers. The most

powerful learning tool is for a learner to see the truth embodied in
another. Prayer is that vehicle God has provided for building our relationship with him.

The requirements given to Israel for corporate prayer apply to today's
church as well:

> If my people who are called by my name will humble themselves and
> pray and seek my face and turn from their wicked ways, then will I hear
> from heaven and will forgive their sin and will heal their land.
>
> [2 Chron. 7:14]

Every church can experience the promise of this scripture. However, its leaders must model humility by declaring their utter dependence on God to lead the church. Leaders must call the church to pray
for extended time periods. They must call prayer meetings and attend
them and lead them. They must provide instructions, methods,
materials, and encouragement to facilitate the corporate prayer.

The prayers must also be intense and persistent. Again, *With Christ
in the School of Prayer* by Andrew Murray is helpful. "Prayer consists
of two parts, has two sides, human and divine. The human is the asking, the divine is the giving. Or, to look at both from the human side,
there is the asking and the receiving—the two halves that make up a
whole. It is as if he would tell us that we are not to rest without an
answer, because it is the will of God, the rule in the Father's family that
every childlike believing petition is granted. If no answer comes, we
are not to sit down in the sloth that calls itself resignation, and suppose that it is not God's will to give an answer. No; there must be something in the prayer that is not as God would have it . . . it is far easier
for the flesh to submit without the answer than to yield itself to be
searched and purfied by the Spirit, until it has learned to pray the prayer
of faith."[8] What Murray is saying is that we should not take no answer
for an answer. We must persist in our prayer efforts.

Leaders can model this mandate. They can teach as they struggle
with God, seek his will, ask and knock, until their prayers are right and
God answers yes or no. Corporate wrestling with God opens up new,
higher levels of spiritual life for any church. The congregation will learn
to pray. As leaders confess their sins, commit to a redirected life, and
permit forgiveness and healing to flow, members of the church will fol-

low. Once this redemptive community begins to grow, the church stands on the verge of insight. And insight opens the door to repentance. Information leads to insight when illuminated by the Holy Spirit. A church viscerally knows when it needs renewal. Something does not seem right. Members are struggling with purpose and mission. They lack motivation to serve on boards, give financially, and bring friends. A sense of sameness and boredom breeds cynicism and a critical spirit. This is what is called "soft data." It is the gut reaction. As a church evaluator, I give a great deal of weight to soft data. The sense that something-is-not-right-here is reason enough for responsible leaders to take action. However, soft data must be joined with hard data. Together they yield the necessary insight.

Let's say I am placed in a pitch black room with a snow white carpet and charged with the task of finding a dark spot on the carpet. I could search for minutes, days, or months and find nothing. Even if I ran my hand over the dark spot hundreds of times, I would have no way of knowing I had found it. Suppose someone comes in and turns on the light. Immediately, I see the dark spot on the snow white carpet! Once the light is on, it is easy. In the same way, I can have the right information but, if I do not have a means of seeing it, then it is useless to me. When the church's mind and eyes are illuminated by the Holy Spirit, he turns on the light, and we get insight. We see it as God sees it.

Repentance

Someone has said, "People love progress but they hate change."

In order for renewal to take place, the church must be brought to the point of repentance. Repentance means to turn away or change one's mind. This linguistic definition is from the Greek word "metanoia," meaning, I change my mind after perceiving the facts. True repentance demands behavioral evidence of a changed mind. In Luke 3:8, Luke mentions "fruit in keeping with repentance." This fruit is behavioral evidence that the sinner has turned away from his previous sin. Scripture does not require perfect behavior, only growth into the proper behavior (see also Acts 26:20).

A logical progression has developed. The church, moved by the proper motive, seeks God through prayer. This intense, persistent corporate prayer yields two things: first, Lovelace's two prerequisites for renewal (awareness of God's holiness and awareness of the depth of man's sin); and second, the promise of 2 Chronicles 7:14.

Being in touch with God permits the church to see itself as God sees it. The members desire to please him out of their pure motive. Now the church is in the repentance mode. The members are ready for change. Prayer leads to insight, insight to repentance, and repentance to change.

Unfortunately, most moments of insight are wasted. Many Spirit-motivated people attend religious meetings, repent of their misdirected lives, and leave the meetings fully intending to change. But, they have been led to believe that the necessary work for change was completed at the meeting: they were delivered; they prayed through; they were saved and sanctified; now, they must go with God. These disciples think they have broken the tape and crossed the finish line. The truth is that confession and repentance only set them on the track to compete. Repentance only marks the starting line for running the race.

When I was nine years old, my family attended a church where revival meetings were regularly held. A common practice during the hymn of invitation was for elders to roam through the room, tapping "the lost" on the shoulder and asking, "Wouldn't you like to go forward tonight?" This was a nightly ritual that would continue for several weeks if God truly blessed. This practice petrified my nine-year-old "lost soul," and I dreaded the fateful tap on my quivering shoulder.

Then it happened; the evangelist himself walked toward me with a sweaty handkerchief in one hand and his big black Bible flopping in the other. He stopped at our pew, stared at me, and reached out and touched me. "Billy," he said, "you know the Lord wants you to go forward, don't you?" "Yes," I said. The next fifteen minutes remain an emotional blur to this day. There was weeping, rejoicing, and a lot of big women hugging me. I had prayed through, I had crossed Jordan, I was saved. No one told me what it meant or what to do next. I had repented and crossed the finish line. That was it; that was enough, they said.

The leadership's role is to provide structure and guidance to the participants. Track lanes must be assigned, rules set for the race, and the location of the finish line made known to all. For this reason, I offer three repentant actions a church can take toward renewal and proof they have indeed heeded the lion's roar.

Basic Spiritual Disciplines

The first is a commitment to the basic spiritual disciplines. There is absolutely no possibility that a church can please God without this commitment. Christians cannot grow properly without regular intake of the Word, a meaningful prayer life, encouragement from others, accountability in the context of community, and personal witness to faith in Christ. Many alternatives are being tried. Leaders now bow at the altars of What Works and Who's Who. These are doomed to fail. There is no way to "wire around" God's rules. Jesus himself, along with Ignatius, Thomas à Kempis, Philipp Spener, John Wesley, Dawson Trotman, Richard Foster, Dallas Willard, and a thousand monks, testify that the basic disciplines form the Christian life support system.

Mastering these basics is the foundation for spiritual health in a renewal setting. Leaders must seek easily accessed means to facilitate the practice of these essentials. The importance of the disciplines in discipleship and leadership will be discussed later, but the most powerful means for convincing the congregation these basics are vital is for the leaders to model them, publicly committing to their practice. Leaders should regularly share their struggles, victories, and failures with their congregations. This creates that redemptive community so essential to honesty, growth, and true spirituality.

Objectivity

The second repentant action I advise is objectivity in diagnosis. In the 1960s, Kenny Rogers led a group called the First Edition. A line from one of their hits was I "need to know what kind of condition my condition is in." Certainly this is true of the contemporary church. And to make an accurate diagnosis of the condition of the church, it must be objective. Proof of repentance is the desire to have a competent, objective diagnosis of the church's condition. The church has sought God's help and asked for him to show them where they have gone wrong. Most often God uses human instruments to communicate his thoughts. I once read about a physician who performed surgery on himself. He attempted to remove his own appendix. What normally was a snap procedure turned out to kill him when he punctured a vital organ. This is the reason I strongly advocate church consultation. There are many qualified consultants who love the church and have given themselves to this work. Many churches have greatly benefited from such consultation and consider it a secondary key to their renewal. Let us look once more at Lovelace's renewal model, this time in the context of primary and secondary keys. His prerequisites are awareness of the holiness of God and the depth of man's sin. This awareness is derived through seeking God by way of prayer, after realizing something is wrong. The primary keys to renewal are justification, sanctification, the indwelling Holy Spirit, and spiritual authority in spiritual conflict. These great truths are part of the commitment to the basic spiritual disciplines. Another way of stating this is that the believer becomes aware of the total salvation package, with all of its rights and privileges. The secondary keys, then, are mission, prayer, community, disenculturation, and theological integration. Although secondary, these are no less important. Secondary simply means they come after and build on the primary issues of spiritual power and the authority of Christ. These secondary issues are as vital to the renewal of the church as the primary. Without them, the church would find itself in the same frustrating predicament as the repentant believer who has no means of applying his repentance.

I'm tired of revival without change, renewal without transformation. If the spiritual energy of renewal isn't channeled into concrete change, the spiritual power will be diffused and absorbed by old, unworkable structures. Then the enthusiasm of the people will wane. You can bang your head against structural barriers for only so long and then you give up.

These issues are broader than simply doing evangelism, or calling the church to pray, or dividing members into small groups. For this reason, it is vital to find a qualified consultant who can help the total ministry of the church by addressing such issues as staffing, programs, facilities, financial priorities, small groups, evangelism, master planning, and leadership selection. Small churches can find help through a variety of means, at low cost. The consultant must love the church and consider his work a calling. Not only should the church look at his experience, it should examine his reputation. He should possess the wisdom to gather soft data by interaction with staff and leaders while on site. And, his consultation should reach deeply into the congregation, extracting objective data from both average and fringe members.

The results of a study by Bob Gilliam yielded the following observation. "Often we are asked, 'Do you ever follow up on churches you have ministered to? What were the results?' Although we do not have a perfect record, we can say that less than five percent of the churches we worked with made no significant progress. About ten percent made some progress after their consultation. This progress could be classified as qualitative, quantitative, or both."[9]

My plea for every church serious about renewal is to get objective consultation and deal with these vital secondary issues. Churches need to invest in the analysis of their effectiveness in light of their purpose and mission. This kind of commitment of time and resources demonstrates a repentant heart on the part of the church.

Teachability

The final repentant action I want to discuss is teachability toward new prescriptive forms. One of life's greatest mysteries is people who know they must change, want the results of a change, yet resist such change. This is very true in parochial institutions like the church. One mature church leader, who fit the above description, expressed this sentiment precisely when he said, "I know we need to change to reach people, but I still oppose the change because it makes me uncomfortable."

Resistance to change is common. And the most common manifestation of such resistance is the confusion between form and function. Function should dictate the form. Form should follow the function. Recently, I asked my wife to prepare a chili dinner for twenty people. She replied firmly, "We can't do that." "Why?" I asked. "We only have ten chili bowls!" she answered. So I went out and bought her twenty matching bowls—white paper bowls. This is a perfect example of form dictating function. Too often our churches behave the same way. The form of Wednesday evening prayer sessions in the chapel dictates God's function. If God is going to function, he must pick up a copy of the schedule and plan to be present at the appointed time.

Conclusion

Before renewal can come, a church must want it. Inherent in wanting renewal is the reason behind wanting it. The first order of business is to evaluate motive. The church is then called to intense, persistent prayer in order to gain insight. This insight opens the door to repentance. Repentance leads to change. And finally comes the prayer for insight. When a church is confronted with making these changes, it must perform empowered by the Spirit. Its members must commit to the basic Christian disciplines in order to lay a foundation. They must humbly submit to an objective diagnosis and apply the prescriptive new forms with a teachable spirit. Then, Christ's promise to fellowship with us in a new and fresh way will become a reality (Rev. 3:20).

Part 2

We Must Develop Principled Training

or

We Don't Want Programmic Junkies

Give me a place to stand, and I will move the earth.

—Archimedes

3

A Theology of Mission

Too many pastors and church leaders plant their philosophical feet firmly in the air; that is, they do not possess a solid, functional theology of mission for the church. The importance of a theology of mission cannot be overstated. While a statement of faith or official doctrinal position is vital to a congregation's reason to exist, it is incomplete without a functional theology of mission. The official doctrinal statement tells us why we are here; the theology of mission addresses the question, "Now, what?" Apart from a disciple's internal struggles with the world, the flesh, and the devil, a lack of theology of mission is the primary reason for church sloth and decline. It manifests itself in a lack of vision and strategy.

Many are asking the wrong questions about the church in North America. They are focusing on models that work, numbers of people, and the unchurched. The inability to exegete culture and minister to baby boomers are not the issues that hurt us the most. The compromised, weak-willed team the evangelical church is putting on the field is the real killer. The right question to address is one that is rarely asked. **What kind of team is the evangelical church putting on the field?** The real test of a pastor's ministry is found in the answer to this probing question. What are his people like Monday through Saturday?

Are they penetrating their networks? Are their lives filled with integrity and power in witness? I will speak more about these issues in later chapters, but for now, we should realize that church leaders must ask and answer these important questions.

Too many graduates exit seminary with brains full of fuzz concerning any theology of mission. They arrive at their assignments loaded with a toolbox of information. They have been instructed on how to deliver a sermon, counsel, officiate at weddings and funerals, visit the sick, and carry out basic administration. While this information is good and can be useful, the major glitch is they know very little about vision, leadership, conflict management, and training others in such areas as ministry skills, strategy, and management.

Pastors and church leaders know they must guide their churches somewhere. Usually, they understand this to mean "win the world" and "equip the saints." But, because they walk in a philosophical "no man's land," they are lost. Without ministry models or principles, they travel from seminar to seminar, reading book after book, in search of something to rescue them.

Knowing I need to lead a church is like knowing I should visit my Uncle Joe for the summer. How I accomplish this is my strategy. I need to take out my road atlas and decide the best route. I need to pick a date. I must determine the cost and where I will stop overnight. I will need to service my car and pack the right clothes. Oh yes, and I must call Uncle Joe to tell him my family is coming.

Many of the leaders with whom I work need to develop such a strategy for their churches. They need to understand that even the Scripture supports strategy. There are biblically based methods for leading a church to its prescribed destination.

A theology of mission is a philosophy of ministry based on scriptural principles. It addresses both the why and how questions. "For God so loved the world that he gave his one and only Son . . ." (John 3:16) answers the why. We do it because God loves us. "Go and make disciples of all nations . . ." (Matt. 28:19) points to the how. God's strategy for telling the world is disciplemaking. A theology of mission must deal with the definition of a disciple as well as the various methods and tools for disciplemaking.

A theology of mission is a principle rather than a methodology. It will work itself out in a program, but we must not mistake the principle for the program. "A principle is a fundamental truth or law . . . not necessarily in detail."[1] If a disciple is going to sustain a lifetime of service to Christ, he must base it on fundamental principles. Principles and methodology can be confused.

On the other hand, sometimes they work hand in hand. For example, one scriptural principle in Matthew 28:19–20 is that you cannot make disciples without accountability. Jesus directed his followers, "teaching them to obey everything I have commanded you." This simple principle can be applied in several ways and contexts, but it must not be confused with any methodology. The principle of multiplication is different. In 2 Timothy 2:2, Paul directs us to "teach men who will be able to teach others also." This law of multiplication is clearly the principle behind reaching the world. At the same time, it is a method: to make multiplication work, one must teach those who can teach others. The method, then, is to instruct willing workers.

From this evolves a strategy for taking a church from point A to point B. Such a theology is derived from a study of who God is and what he wants. For example, Matthew 28:18–19 says, "All authority in heaven and on earth has been given to me. Therefore go and make disciples of all nations. . . ." The identity of God—a theology of being—and the mission done on his behalf—a theology of doing—are connected. The two cannot be separated.

Imagine the quality of leadership of the over 150,000 evangelical churches in the United States if the principals worked through and developed a theology of mission! Think about the impact of such churches, where members own the vision, can understand and articulate the goals, and then launch an aggressive program based on a well-understood, biblically based philosophy of ministry. It is my prayer and mission to help churches do this. The serious challenge is to teach church leadership how. This means practically reaching them, training them, and making such training stick.

4

Working Models

hile in a college gym class, I was asked to execute several moves on gymnastic rings. The teacher told me to grab hold, hang from the rings, and pull myself into several unusual positions. Neither I nor the rest of the class had any idea what he meant. The teacher finally demonstrated the moves for us. Although that did not make it any easier, it did give me a mental image of what was required.

We must first teach leaders to have a theology of mission. Then they can develop a mental image of how to accomplish the mission through working models. Our training must set forth the principles of leadership, people development, and evangelism, just as Paul espoused for the corporate church in Ephesians 4:11–16. Working models provide the illustration of the principle. If the principle can be identified, and then illustrated by a method, the average learner can "get a fix" on the principle more quickly. When a working model is not principle-based, a serious flaw emerges. The model falters because methods must change with culture, and a model that is not principle-based will not be adaptable. I would submit that **starting with principles rather than models is the key to building leaders.** If you want short-term results, rely on models. If you desire long-term results, and a continual stream of emerging, working models, begin with a foundation of philosophical principles.

A prime example of this is the Sunday evening evangelistic service, once the cutting edge for a church to draw non-Christians. During the nineteenth century, most people did not own gas lights, so they attended the Sunday evening service to watch the lights burn. Innovative church leaders employed this for evangelism, but such a method would not work today. The principle at work here, however, is to gain access to the people we want to evangelize. Unfortunately, too many churches do not understand the difference between the principle and the method.

To understand effective training, we must understand effective learning. This is the starting point. My personal observation has been that church leaders learn by pursuing working models. Working models successful in numerical growth build a strong magnetic force field that attracts eager church leaders. There is nothing particularly wrong or unnatural about this. However, there is a serious danger in leaders attempting to squeeze, push, and shove someone else's working model into their context.

I am distressed by the mad rush to adopt successful working models. Today there is a dangerous groveling at this altar of pragmatism within the evangelical church. Working models are useful; in fact, we must have them, but we must offer them only after the principles are developed, and they must be based upon those principles.

Principles First

Sometimes, a pastor calls or writes me. "Bill, it didn't work for me," he will say. "I tried your stuff. My board resisted, and my congregation didn't respond." Each of these disappointed leaders made the same mistake: They took my working model and attempted to impose it on their system. Working models almost always fail when they are plopped down in a different context. This is why I repeatedly warn all interested parties that they must write their own principled scripts. I will give them the principles; they must implement them within their own context.

For long-term effect, leadership must become convinced, scripturally, that the new direction is valid. Often, eager leaders confuse those methods and practices that are culturally acceptable in the creator's context with what would work in their own. For example, a "user friendly," seeker-sensitive worship service in San Francisco is not necessarily "user friendly" in Ping Pong, Minnesota. Such issues as training leadership, streamlining committees, reducing services, and changing target audiences on Sunday morning should not be confused with principles that can be inserted without any changes.

Paul said, "Follow my example, as I follow the example of Christ" (1 Cor. 11:1). Earlier in the Corinthian letter, he uses Timothy as an example of what he means by imitation. "He will remind you of my way of life in Christ Jesus, which agrees with what I teach everywhere in every church" (1 Cor. 4:17). Paul passed on a set of principles to be taught in every church. They were the synthesis, or philosophy, of ministry that spread throughout his church network. He was not passing on personality or gifts or methods. The pastoral Epistles are a testament to Paul and Timothy's differences. No two people could have been more different. No two people could have been more alike, either. Yet, Timothy is exhorted to "entrust [these things] to reliable men who will also be qualified to teach others" (2 Tim. 2:2). Paul urged others to imitate him.

The distressing truth about contemporary, pastoral role models is that, in large part, they are non-reproducible. Men presented at conferences are often charismatic and highly gifted. They have a greater measure of gift than the average person. They can inspire ordinary men to action, and they are often worth hearing and imitating. I thank God for such servants; we can learn much from them. The problem, however, is that Scripture teaches us to be committed to reproduction, and these role models cannot be reproduced. While we can catch their spirit and passion for God and mission, impersonating them can lead to frustration and guilt.

And here lies the conflict. Ninety-five percent of the time, the listeners cannot do what the speaker does, no matter how godly or hardworking they may be. The danger, then, is one of impersonation rather than imitation. To impersonate means one is trying to be someone he is not, by doing violence to his genetic code. This is an ugly contortion of emotion. In popular culture, the most pathetic manifestation of this is the Elvis impersonators. Impersonating a popular evangelical luminary is not as pathetic, but it can be more devastating. As church leaders, we are to imitate a set of principles, not a gift or a personality or a context or any other nontransferable, nonreproducible trait.

Spiritual Character

An often forgotten factor in church growth and renewal is the spiritual character of the creative personality. It is superficial to consider the highly gifted only "flash and dash." I have been pleasantly surprised by the commitment of many luminaries to basic spiritual disciplines. Many of these men have a close walk with God. It is easy for us to focus on their talents, forgetting their struggles, perseverance, and willingness to empty themselves for Christ. The danger for church leaders looking to benefit from working models is to neglect the importance of spiritual character in the process. God uses people who are submitted to him and desire to promote his kingdom and his person. Everyone can develop spiritual character, but it does not come with the working model. Packages often read "batteries not included"; this is the case with working models. Rather than anointing just an idea, God anoints a person with passion and heart, combined with giftedness.

Benefit of Working Models

A group of church leaders assembled for training come from diverse situations. The pastor from a rural congregation of seventy-five and the pastor from a suburban church of two thousand have major differences. Yet they share the same allegiance to Scripture, and they share a basic set of principles to govern their ministries. It is their respective responsibilities to contextualize these principles in their particular situations. The only responsible and effective way to train for the long-term is to teach on a principled basis.

Working models can benefit church leaders. A highly motivated leader can adapt models, glean the principles or ideas, and make them work. When a model is principle-based, then change is welcomed and actually improves the principled application. Most people learn interactively. Once they see something working in one form, they can take it and contextualize it for their purpose. Church leaders who can rejoice with the success of their brethren are the ones who can benefit best. Spending a few days in a megachurch with a large staff can greatly refresh a small church pastor. It can offer him hope. If he will identify principles and contextualize to his context and style, great things can take place. His small church can make a real difference in its community.

Contemporary working models developed by Rick Warren, Frank Tillapaugh, Bill Hybels, John MacArthur, Dave Galloway, Jack Hayford, Randy Pope, and others have given church leaders a mighty boost in the right direction. Consider the positive changes in the church over the last twenty years that have resulted from contemporary catalytic models. MacArthur, Swindoll, and Hocking lead the Pulpit-centered Bible Teaching Model. Bill Hybels and Rick Warren direct the Life Situational Entrepreneurial Model. John Wimber pulls the church toward Signs and Wonders. Peter Wagner moves the church toward Prayer; while George Barna presses forward with Market-driven Evangelism. Evangelical leaders, such as Dale Galloway and his Cell-based Church and Jack Hayford and his Reformation in Worship, are moving to the forward position. Within the Southern Baptist denomination, Ed Young and Frank Jackson demonstrate new methods. Other significant forces abound. Both Calvary Chapels and the Disciplemaking Movement are now forging vital inroads into the local church.

I adapt better than I create. I have forged much of what I believe by dialoguing with those who were making the ideas work. I have extracted principles and used them. Over the years, I have refined both the principles and the methods. God has graciously allowed me to develop a training network in an attempt to help churches. I started T-NET, as we call it, in response to churches' inquiries about disciplemaking. People would call and ask if they could spend a few days with us to observe our work. We spent hours on the phone. After a while, we simply did not have the time. My experience was a smaller version of what other working models had done, but this led to a training network that is now international in scope.

Principles provide the foundation for effective working models. And fresh expressions of those principles grab a church's attention. Working models offer a kind of positive lodestar to which interested parties can run for hope, inspiration, and instruction. Such models spearhead renewal and are essential in order for Christ to rebuild his church. In fact, a successful working model for disciplemaking principles is one of Christ's objectives on this earth. The Lord can hold up a contemporary mirror before each church and say this one is good. What can you use? May God multiply effective working models!

5

Principle-based Training

 number of philosophical mentors and writers have influenced my commitment to teach leaders at the principle level. I particularly like Peter Drucker's "Way of Thinking," in which he develops a pyramid of three steps or phases on how people reach breakthrough and lasting behavioral change.[2]

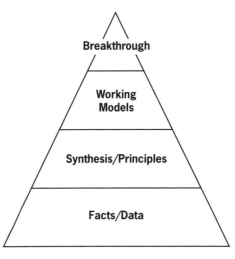

Peter Drucker's "Way of Thinking" are notes developed by Bob Buford. Used by permission of Drucker and Buford.

This pyramid starts at the Facts/Data level; it is crucial for one to find the correct set of facts and data. Drucker's second step is Synthesis, or what I call the crafting of principles and philosophy. A working model is developed from this. This working model then provides the confidence and the proof that the principles are valid. Finally comes Breakthrough, or behavioral change.

I would like to alter the pyramid slightly for my purposes.

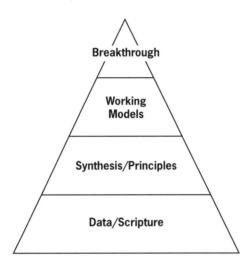

This model fundamentally agrees with Drucker's—my changes are mainly in nomenclature. The first step on this altered pyramid is Data/Scripture. The second is Synthesis, which yields a philosophy of ministry. Based on this principled philosophy of ministry, a working model is developed. My fourth step corresponds with Drucker's: Breakthrough and behavioral change. This learning process can work in any context, personal or corporate. The point is that the process works in revitalization of churches and in church planting as well.

If the church is to be renewed, leaders must be taught. Drucker's pyramid communicates steps to learning and behavioral change. I conclude from Scripture, with a helpful boost from Drucker, that true commitment focuses on scripturally based data, refined by life synthesis into a philosophy of ministry or principles. Regardless of the teaching methodology, a principled leadership is the best leadership.

I would now like to introduce a third pyramid structure.[3]

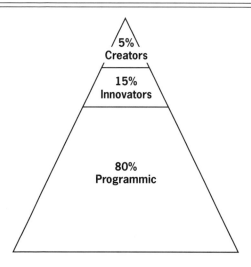

Wagner's Observation of Clergy. C. Peter Wagner, "Church Growth Eyes." Used by permission.

In this model, C. Peter Wagner observes that, whether by interaction or internal reflection, only 5 percent of clergy create new ideas, concepts, or expressions. Another 15 percent are innovative, advocating change and effectively adapting what the creative think to make it work better. The largest category of clergy are the programmic 80 percent who rarely create or innovate. They do not operate on a principle basis; rather, they need concrete, planned steps before them in order to work on an expression of ministry.

Now, let us compare Drucker's altered pyramid with Wagner's.

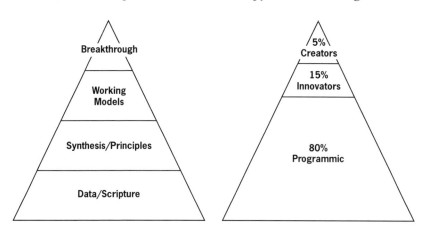

This pyramid interface creates a dilemma. A successful training model should address the different approaches in Wagner's pyramid while accomplishing the needed stages of Drucker's. To start teaching leaders, we must begin at Drucker's first two levels. However, Wagner's pyramid indicates that 80 percent of the clergy are programmic and will flock toward the working model. In my estimation, over the long run working models create sinkholes, which will eventually give way. I offer the following conclusions about this pyramid interface.

Effective Training

Creators and innovators need a starting point that is distinct from the programmic. Therefore, we should start this upper 20 percent with a scripturally based philosophy of ministry. Since they are less inclined to be model dependent and want to make it on their own, creators and innovators respond best to principles.

The majority of entrepreneur pastors fall into the 5 percent category of creators. Creators get a whiff of an idea; they take it, improve it, and do better than the originator. This group needs less formal training than the other 99 percent, and particularly less than the 80 percent programmic. They do, however, need some training and accountability. Their training must be different in order to attract them. One of the challenges in reaching the "K" church pastor, who pastors 1,000 or more, is motivating him to attend any meeting where he is not the headliner.

According to Elmer Towns, about 4,000 "K" churches exist in the United States today out of the approximately 400,000 churches nationwide. Pastors of such churches are usually around fifty years old, talented, highly gifted, and hardworking. Most denominational meetings are marked by the absence of any "K" church pastors. When they would be simply conferees, many evangelical luminaries have stayed away from meetings with fellow clergy. Older "K" church pastors have discipled newer "K" church pastors to stay away from the traditional training meetings. It is an ego issue. The rationalization is that other members of the "K Club" stay away, so the new member must stay away, too.

The Leadership Network, led by Fred Smith Jr. and Bob Buford, has attempted to encourage this group by holding conferences where they can interact with one another rather than listen to a series of lectures. Smith and Buford believe these pastors will be more encouraged by interaction and will reach some sort of communal "critical mass"; i.e., there will be new ideas and a conceptual breakthrough. "K Club" members have the highest respect for one another. They believe they can learn more from one another than from those who have not walked in their shoes. By common experience and a sense of brotherhood, they will meet for a "critical mass" experience. (I am happy to say that the baser attitudes among "K" church pastors are truly no more prevalent than with other pastors. Their temptations and needs, apart from the common fare, just happen to be different.)

In renewing the church at large, the "K Club" is not the primary training target. It forms a meager 1 percent of the pastoral population. The objective is to get all leaders operating on a principle basis. This is vital for a lifelong commitment to a scripturally based philosophy of ministry. Such a philosophy transcends the cultures and contexts and permits a person to make disciples anywhere. The end point is the same; it's the starting point that is different.

The programmic group is no more or less intelligent, spiritual, or educated than the creators and innovators. They are simply differently "wired" by the Creator. The programmic are the majority of clergy. They feel comfortable learning about and evaluating what is working. They like to paint by numbers. Principles and philosophical ministry statements are too theoretical, but working models attract them. An important window of opportunity exists early in the programmic's ministry when he is in search of some solid philosophical ground. This is the time to construct a theology of mission under them.

Principles and the Programmic Thinker

Let's assume that we have successfully motivated the programmic thinker to attend a training conference. He is there because he believes we have a road-tested, working model. Our first act is to satisfy his appetite for the utilitarian model. This model should be taught in total, along with ample opportunity to ask the "how" questions. Our objective, however, is to start with the "why" questions. If the attendees do not ask the questions, then the teacher must. Our objective is to provide a theology of mission that will serve programmic thinkers all their lives. It is only a secondary objective to provide them with a working model because it is culturally limited and possesses a short life span. Like a ship at sea without engine or sails, it sits on changing tides, slowly taking on water, with only a matter of time until it sinks. Although they were attracted by the program, what these programmic thinkers really need are principles. With as much capacity to understand principles as the creators and innovators, still they do not see them and are not attracted to them unless the principles are explained and tied to practical success. When these thinkers have opportunities to process program and principle, they catch it, and it is theirs for life. This requires a process, however. It is not enough to understand principle as illustrated in program on a theoretical basis alone. For the programmic thinker, the principles must be experienced. Then they feel true ownership and conviction concerning the theology of mission that rests on those principles.

This process requires two years to reach the convictional level. Seminars, books, and conferences will not get programmic pastors to the desired destination. In order to reach the 80 percent with a scripturally based theology of mission, a more comprehensive process must be crafted. Jesus himself gave the six-step teaching method: 1) tell them what, 2) tell them why, 3) show them how, 4) do it with them, 5) let them do it, and 6) deploy them.[4] It may seem extreme to claim two years in order to reach Drucker's Breakthrough, but the principles can be internalized only through life experience, and it takes time for the consistent practice of the principles to yield results.

Breakthrough is defined as the successful completion of the process depicted by the pyramid. It means the learner has built an effective learning model, based on a synthetic—or blended—biblical foundation. The programmic pastor starts with a working model, moves on to specifically related principles, and then practices the principles until the convictions are built. When the principle model does start working, the leader moves from a theoretician's conviction to a practitioner's conviction.

The training process is vital. A minimum of two years is spent discipling church leaders in accountability. You cannot make disciples without accountability, and you cannot have accountability without structure.

A Three-Pronged Strategy

Any training model for returning the church to its disciplemaking roots requires a three-pronged strategy. First, the local church level must model the disciplemaking strategy. Next, seminaries must teach the theology of mission. And third, it all must be reinforced on the field.

The local church must model the disciplemaking strategy. The most convincing teaching model for disciplemaking is the local church. Going beyond the tell-them-what-and-why of academia to the crucial stages of show-them-how and do-it-with-them is the best kind of training. It supersedes seminaries, seminars, training networks, videos, and literature.

When an entrepreneurial leader develops a flagship church, the local church model is at its best. A flagship church is designed to embody the principles and reproduce itself many times over. Young leaders willing to raise their own support are good candidates for church planting. An intern church planter lives and works with the flagship and is deployed to reproduce that model in a nearby community. The church planter remains accountable to the mother church and interacts weekly on strategy, personal spiritual disciplines, and other issues in order to encourage his success. The flagship can eventually weave a complete network of kindred churches in the community. It would not be extraordinary for ten congregations to emerge from one flagship.

When a model works well and is built on disciplemaking principles, then reproduce it and multiply it, again and again! This particular model does work well, and today wise leaders are combing the national countryside to find those who can serve as first-strike, flagship pastors with a passion for disciplemaking and church planting.

Christ modeled Christocentric disciplemaking outside the organizational infrastructure. Churchocentric disciplemaking[5] is the successful application by the apostles of what Christ taught them. Churchocentric describes the revealed application in Acts and the Epistles. Its apex was the expression of Paul's work at Ephesus. I mention it here because it is crucial to a successful model. It is not difficult to see Christocentric disciplemaking taking place. Navigators, Campus Crusade for Christ, and many other "parachurch" groups—or mission groups focusing the Great Commission on one segment of the population—offer several models. However, it is rare to find churchocentric disciplemaking models in local churches.

I am reminded of the words of Oliver Wendell Holmes, "I wouldn't give a fig for simplicity on this side of complexity, but I would give my life for simplicity on the other side of complexity." To find working disciplemaking models in local churches is to find a successful integration of disciplemaking and local church infrastructure. This is simplicity that has made its way through, emerging victorious on the other side of complexity.

Let us look at the five basic distinctives to apostolic application of Christ's disciplemaking training. Once again, it is vital to understand that the apostles successfully translated Christ's principles into different structures. The five distinctives that Christ taught and modeled are:

1. Leadership: from Christ leading twelve, to a leadership team leading a congregation.
2. Guidance: from Christ speaking the unmistakable will of God, to a leadership team employing prayer, Scripture, counsel, discernment, and congregational input in order to determine God's will.
3. Training: from Christ instructing a few, to multi-leveled training of many.
4. Outreach: from Christ and the apostles doing individual, direct evangelism, to evangelism based on spiritual gifts directed through natural networks.
5. Pastoral Care: from Christ knowing and meeting all needs, to the mutual caring for one another through the gifts of the body.

Those committed to historic discipleship have been frustrated with the local church. I have spoken to many veterans who emerged from the discipling movement of the 1950s and are skeptical that disciplemaking can work in the local church context. These faithful followers of Christ have poured their lives into others and have influenced thousands for Christ. Yet, they are cynical toward the church and tell me that I have "saddled a dead horse." They hope they are wrong, and I am right. They wish me "Godspeed," but they believe I will fail in my quest to return the church to its disciplemaking roots.

These veterans have spent their lives trying to push a round peg into a square hole. What too many have missed is the transition from the Gospels to the Epistles, from Christ leading the twelve to the apostles leading the church, from the Christocentric model to the churchocentric, disciplemaking model. This difference is the key to returning the church to its disciplemaking roots. *It's got to be churchocentric to work!*

This difference is also the key breakthrough, philosophically, for renewing the church and making its obedience to the Great Commission a possibility. Because churchocentric disciplemaking is a round peg in a round hole, it is like finding the missing link. It can make discipleship a normal local-church experience. We do not need models driven by prevailing markets and consumer desires. We need churchocentric models driven by God's values as revealed in Scripture. If churches are to become disciplemaking, they must be Word-driven. If prevailing markets and consumer desires intersect with God's directions, we have a happy moment. May God give us these!

Seminaries must teach a theology of mission. The theological seminary still controls the basic belief systems of the church. The faculty are charged with protecting the theological integrity of the particular denomination or segment of the church they serve. They are custodians of vital information and wisdom and must pass this on to their students. A good seminary education will equip students for about 40 to 50 percent of what they will face. Other professional schools, such as medicine and law, work in controlled environments where hands-on work is practiced. Seminaries, however, are seriously hamstrung because sending an intern into a local church is sending him into an uncontrolled environment. Each church teaches something different, and often teaches more wrong than right. Since this academic setting has limitations, the logical question is: What can a seminary do about teaching a theology of mission?

The first thing it can do is build convictions. A seminary is called a seminary because it is to be a seminal experience. Seminaries are supposed to plant seeds that will grow healthy convictions over time. The faculty make strong impressions on the supple minds of the young, so strong that, for the first decade of a graduate's ministry, he often seeks approval for his work from his favorite faculty member or members. Therefore, it is the faculty's responsibility to plant disciplemaking seeds in its students. The seminary faculty must be committed to more than formal training. It must take an interest in the students themselves, in order to plant ideological disciples.

Many seminaries are now in decline. As the late Dean Inge stated, "He who marries the spirit of the age will soon become a widower." The seminaries that are now growing will decline unless they come to terms with reality. This reality is the present educational model. The day of the pulpit-centered, professional pastor is over; the day of the mission-minded, disciple-maker pastor has come. The professional pastor and the institutionalized local church have become dysfunctional. A seminary education that trains for the old model is dysfunctional as well.

This does not mean that theology is declining. Theology will become more important as we move into the next century. The winds of cultural change will blow away every culturally fixed ideology unless the theology is firmly grounded. During the 1980s, we witnessed the rise and fall of the religious right. During the early 1990s, we witnessed the remarkable collapse of communism.

I recently heard a speaker relate that twenty-nine systematic theologies are currently being written. Yet, surprisingly, all of these theologies are being written by neo-orthodox theologians or liberals. Evangelical scholars need to get busy.

The changes in seminary training must come in the practical theology departments. While many seminaries are staffed by outstanding preachers and experienced counselors, their departments are normally weak in a functional theology of mission. At least one third of the faculty should be local-church strategists who can train others in church planting and revitalization. This will require resisting inflexible accreditation associations and their peccadillos, and stocking practical theology departments with proven strategists. I am not advocating a full rebellion—only a slight one. Just as public schools would benefit by filling faculty vacancies with successful people from the marketplace, seminaries should make room for effective leaders by requiring each master of divinity student to study a theology of mission.

We must reinforce the training in the field. Pastors spend three years in seminary and thirty years on the field. Most denominations direct nearly all of their financial support for pastoral training to seminaries. My denomination alone allocates ten million dollars annually to the support of the seminary. Yet we have no established continuing education program. To overcome this huge imbalance, I suggest that we establish training networks. The objective of such networks is to produce and multiply healthy, reproducing, intentional, disciplemaking churches. This must be our objective because it is Christ's objective for the church (Matt. 28:19–20). Presently, I am in the midst of building an international training network to train leadership teams. I will discuss the details of the training network in the next chapter. But it is a war! The enemy resists the most at the greatest point of obedience. The Great Commission encounters the Great Resistance. Satan does not want our churches to take the Great Commission seriously because he knows it holds the key to world evangelization. In the past decade, I have engaged the enemy on several fronts, with the most basic battleground at the local-church level. Another battlefront has been in the area of contemporary literature, which must be contextualized to the local church. J. I. Packer stated, "Every movement of ideas needs its own literature." (I hope to provide some of that literature.)

A third enemy attack has been against seminars for pastors. We are now producing workbooks and videos in an attempt to help pastors transform their churches into intentional, disciplemaking centers. A fourth battlefront is the seminary.

The efforts to counter Satan's attacks in these areas still lack the depth and longevity needed to be successful. That means that the church's most profound needs will go unmet because many pastors and church leaders are not able to meet them without help. These needs are hands-on, ongoing help and the training of clergy and laity together as teams.

This brings us back to training. I am convinced that true transformation requires ongoing training for at least two years. Additionally, there must be accountability, or "teeth," in the process. Laity must be involved at the source of the training level. Most often, they are engaged only on a secondary level. When this happens, too much is lost in the translation, and the training lacks ownership and punch. The pastor is the key, but changes must be lay-driven in order to have a long life.

The Training Network

The training network employs four primary principles. These converge to form effective training.

1. *A balanced approach of centralized training and on-site consultation.* Both are necessary to bring about the breakthrough churches need. Only a centralized approach permits the use of a few good trainers. It also allows participants to learn from others who are encountering the same problems and finding workable solutions. The training network participants gather in a central location in their area, several times over the course of two years. Because unique difficulties are often encountered in individual churches, the training network provides the use of an on-site consultant to help in leadership development, evangelism, the creation of small groups, and other areas. Some habits and techniques are best learned by watching and modeling others. The on-site consultant is equipped to train church leaders in techniques and to serve as a model.

2. *Process-oriented training rather than event-oriented training.* The training network is not a seminar; it is a training process. Unlike most information-oriented seminars, this training shows pastors and leaders how to develop new habits. The objective is behavioral change that leads to Word-driven people, development, and evangelism. This takes time. It also requires opportunities to try, fail, try again, and finally succeed in a setting that provides resources, expertise, and support. Therefore, the training process is spread over twenty-four months and includes six meetings at a central location. The process-oriented approach greatly enhances the probability of success. The real key to success, however, is the determination of each leadership team to make it work.

3. *The training of leadership teams, not just pastors.* Seventy percent of the training network participants are laity. It is essential that the vision be lay-driven. This is team building around a philosophy of ministry and a common plan, providing lay ownership and giving pastors advocates who believe in the church's future. When a seminar trains one person, usually the pastor, the pastor returns home facing both an information gap and possible resistance from his leaders. Even without resistance, valuable time elapses before his leaders can be trained. In contrast, the training network trains an entire team of leaders (five minimum) from each church. These people are immediately ready to lead in disciplemaking, with the pastor. This team provides a valuable base of support when opposition arises.

4. *Specialized training in various tracks.* An effective training network must be philosophically united with its objective. Its objective

must be to produce disciplemaking churches. A great harvest comes when a planter nourishes the roots and focuses on the basic issues that bring health. Everything a church needs is resident in the undiscipled members of the church. By focusing on the root system of the church, the leader will get an enduring, multiplied harvest.

My ministry limits the basic tracks to three: (1) leadership, (2) evangelism, (3) education. These three tracks touch the major core issues of local church life. Whenever possible, the tracks divide participants according to church size in order to increase the relevance of the training.

For this reason, we have resisted the temptation to touch and train in every area. I am often asked why we do not do track training in such areas as support groups, women's ministry, marketplace ministry, singles, single parents, twelve-step recovery groups, or world missions. My answer is that these ministries are manifestations of disciplemaking. They are the things that developed disciples do. If we do not start with the basics and build, these ministries will either not emerge, will be short-lived, or will need constant promotion to live. When church members are trained in disciplemaking, some of these ministries will follow naturally and will grow.

The Results

There are three major results that grow from developing a principled approach to training leadership.

The first is a *greatly improved local-church ministry*. To monitor the vital signs for this, I would ask the following questions. Are the leaders unified around the concepts? Are they working together to implement the strategy churchwide? Additionally, are they personally modeling the goals and objectives they have set? Has evangelism increased, both corporately and individually? Is the church creatively reaching out and effectively assimilating new converts? What is happening in small groups? Are they providing environments to encourage the basic spiritual disciplines and higher commitment? Have they successfully implemented their training? In other words, has the local church ministry greatly improved?

The second is that *new disciplemaking churches are being planted*. To monitor the signs for this, I would ask these questions. Are the leaders recruiting progressive young men who want to pioneer new model churches as beachheads until there is a saturation of evangelistic, disciplemaking church plants? Do they have a grass-roots network, or outposts, manned by well-trained church planters? Are the new churches committed to disciplemaking principles? Have they been able to increase their production? Is there real growth in the church through conversions, or are they merely reconfiguring those already saved?

The third result is *the production of thousands of disciplemaking advocates*. The training network's greatest contribution is the raising up of thousands of trained disciple-makers. The success of the network depends on the apprenticeship concept. The original faculty led the first generation. They are then replaced by hundreds of apprentices, who in turn train others. The network grows by multiplication. And the sites increase from a few, to hundreds, to thousands. Success is measured by the number of people trained in all basic tracks.

To monitor the vital signs, church leaders can address many of the same questions probed in the areas above. Are the leaders unified around the concepts? Are they working together to implement the strategy church-wide? Are they personally modeling the goals and objectives they have set? Has evangelism increased, both corporately and individually? Is the church creatively reaching out and effectively assimilating new converts? What is happening in small groups? Are they providing environments to encourage the basic spiritual disciplines and higher commitment? In other words, have they successfully implemented their training?

The ultimate goal is for the training to become more decentralized and as close to the grass roots as possible. The training's value is measured by its ability to transform the person in the pew from a spectator to a minister, or from a hearer to a doer. Any mission worth giving oneself to should outlive its participants. The training network's purpose is to implant these convictions in hundreds of thousands of church leaders throughout the world. Knowing that thousands will spend eternity in heaven instead of hell because of the training network makes all the work worthwhile.

Conclusion

We must act now to restore the church to its disciplemaking roots. This can only be done by training church leaders in a theology of mission, based on scriptural principles. Building on this foundation rather than on the foundation of working models is the key to building effective leadership. We must first teach leaders a theology of mission. Then they will follow up with working models. If the church is to be renewed, leaders must be taught. Teaching methods vary depending on the learning style. Regardless of the teaching methodology, a principled leadership is the best leadership. We must teach leaders to obey the commands of Christ as they relate to leading the church in mission and strategy. Training must set forth the principles of leadership, people development, and evangelism. Working models provide illustration of these principles. When a model is principle-based, change is welcomed and actually improves the principled application.

Training models for returning the church to its disciplemaking roots require that the local church model the disciplemaking strategy; that seminaries teach a theology of mission; and finally, that all of it is reinforced on the field. The reinforcement can be accomplished effectively through the flagship church model and training networks. I believe that the training network, the churchocentric, disciplemaking technique, is the missing link to renewal in today's churches.

I pray that we can convince and train leaders from every nation that making disciples is the key to evangelizing the world. If we can, and I think we can, Christ will be glorified in his church.

Part **3**

We Must Transform Existing Leadership

or

If We Can Teach an Elephant to Dance, We Can Teach a Deacon to Lead

6

The Problem

hurch leaders are like trained elephants. "They both have learned through conditioning. Trainers shackle young elephants with heavy chains to deeply embedded stakes. In that way the elephant learns to stay in its place. Older elephants never try to leave even though they have the strength to pull the stake and move beyond. Their conditioning limits their movements with only a small metal bracelet around their foot—attached to nothing."[1] Elephants are capable of doing more than they think. Most people believe elephants cannot dance, but what people believe is irrelevant. What do elephants believe? And, what do elephant trainers believe? These are relevant!

Like elephants, many church leaders believe they are chained—the only issue is how long the chain is. Just as an elephant can be taught to dance, a church leader can be taught to lead. Once the church leader realizes he is limited only by faith and perception, he can soar to great heights.

One of the most urgent questions asked by pastors today is how to transform existing leadership. They bemoan the fact they do not know what to do. Leaders are entrenched, unwilling to change. They are not spiritually motivated or ministry-minded. What should be the greatest strength of any church is, nationwide, the greatest frustration and battleground. I have listened to many pastors state their anguish with tears in their eyes. "If only I could get a new group of leaders," they cry. "If only they would let me lead. If only they would be on my side." Lay leaders respond: "If only our pastor would lead. If only he would inspire us. If only . . . if only . . . if only . . ."

The great irony is that pastors and lay leaders desire the same thing: effective churches. This stalemate has stalled many churches. Breaking the pattern is the greatest challenge for the church of the 1990s, and beyond.

Church renewal is an issue of leadership. If a way is not found for church leadership teams to break the bondage of ineffective leadership models, there will be no church renewal. This is how crucial the renewal of existing leaders is to the cause of Christ. If renewal is to take place, it must begin at the leadership level. Poor lay leadership is linked to poor pastoral leadership. Pastors are frustrated, and lay people are uninspired. Pastors are being fired, and lay people are becoming disenchanted. All are dropping out in greater numbers than ever. They are angry and bitter and have sworn off future church involvement. Some of the happiest people I know are elated to be ex-church leaders.

Leaders make or break any plan, program, or attempt to renew a congregation. If the leaders are open to and seriously pursue personal renewal, then the congregation will follow. The problem is that, as a whole, church leaders are not leading. Many will not lead. Some cannot lead. And others do not know how to lead.

Leaders Who Will Not Lead

The group of leaders who will not lead is composed of managers, technicians, and those lacking convictions and courage. These are the finger-in-the-air types, who lead by consensus or public opinion. Most often, these leaders ask what the people will do if . . . Those in this group may have leadership potential, ambition, and even know-how, but they are not willing to risk criticism and loss of friendships when faced with an unpopular decision. These leaders are more like the congressmen who function essentially as emissaries for special-interest groups. They see themselves as congregational representatives rather than leaders called by God and governed by Scripture. This is one of the church's most worldly characteristics. The enemy has invaded the church with a secular polity borrowed from the American political system.

Leaders Who Cannot Lead

One of the contemporary church's greatest mistakes is placing non-leaders into leadership positions. Recent church history testifies to our placing those who are faithful and available in leadership roles, without considering their suitability for the task. According to Peter Drucker, the most important consideration in personnel selection is the assignment. Once this has been determined, the next job is to find the person who is gifted and called to fill the assignment. Because so few churches know about or believe in the principle of selectivity, their leadership appointments present a fundamental glitch in God's economy.

What does a pastor do with leaders who cannot lead? Regardless of spiritual qualities or willing hearts, such a group is like ten pygmies becoming a basketball team in the National Basketball Association. It plays hard, gets beaten regularly, and does not enjoy the process.

Leaders Who Don't Know How to Lead

When leaders do not know how to lead because of lack of training and vision, most churches fail to face the problem. In most churches, any prerequisite training program for leadership is fiercely opposed. Fifty years ago, most of America was rural and the churches small. Everyone knew everything about everybody. The informal, soft-data approach based on relationships was used, and it worked well. In fact, it still works well in those types of communities.

Leadership Selection

What worked in rural America has failed miserably in our metropolitan areas. Rural "hangovers," like increasing board size in direct relation to church membership, have multiplied committees and bureaucracy. This has formed administrative bottlenecks (such as taking three months to make three decisions). Today we live in an individualistic, impersonal, cut-flower society where soft data is scarce. The modern church must use more formal means, or hard data, for leadership selection, which is objective and provides some security from the pathologies of a broken culture.

There are four functional reasons for the problems within today's church leadership.

Executives Rather Than Disciples

We have failed to install the basic spiritual disciplines as part of the leadership motif. Too few leadership teams are dominated by the members' commitment to Bible study, Scripture memorization, personal and corporate prayer, and meaningful accountability in such areas as finance, morality, family, and personal witness. Too few evangelical church board members regularly witness.

The institutional environment of local churches teaches leaders a different set of values. What matters is efficient management of committees and budget. How to run meetings, file reports, and write and execute policy are the important things. In other words, the mechanics of ministry have become the ministry. The tools of facilitation have taken on a life of their own.

These issues are critical to an effective church. Fewer meetings, shorter meetings, and more productive meetings are keys to unlocking the church's ability to minister. In many churches today, leaders do not need spiritual skills or character. For the skills that are used, the training could be done better in the business community. In fact, in many cases the entire set of skills for church leadership could be accessed without the church lifting a hand to train. This is not a good trend.

The result is a secularization of the spiritual organization. In far too many evangelical churches, the real power lies not in spiritual leaders, but in the administrative leadership. An example of this can be found where the deacon boards have become the spiritual leaders rather than remaining subservient to their churches' top leadership boards. This hierarchy of placing administrative leadership above the spiritual leadership communicates plenty. It perpetuates the philosophy that the real, or material, world is more vital and real than the spiritual world. You value that to which you give your best.

In this case, the church values the maintenance and efficient management of the institution. This has led to devaluing spiritual disciplines as prerequisites for leadership. No wonder any attempt to change the leadership culture is fiercely opposed. If leaders are told they must become disciples, they must share their faith, and they must get involved in people's lives as teachers, counselors, and spiritual leaders, they feel threatened because they've received no training. Naturally they oppose any attempt to oust them or make them look inadequate, so many respond that they've been disciples for years. How can anyone tell them they're not good enough to be leaders anymore! They argue tradition and policy in an attempt to deflect the discussion away from those personal, spiritual issues cutting so close to the bone.

If the purpose of the church is to make disciples, then the top board of the church must become proven disciples. The real spiritual authority rests in the modeling of the church's values, as seen in its leaders. The church's mandate is to make disciples—let the world make executives.

Politicians Rather Than Ministers

The church's focus should be ministerial, not political. It is disappointing to ask most church chairmen/moderators to describe their roles. They will tell you about chairing meetings and fielding complaints, petitions, and late-night phone calls. They will tell you how tired they are. They will talk about discouragement, how disappointed they are in several congregational members, and the rough and tumble political battle. One church chairman named John told me that the time he spent as congregational administrative head nearly ruined his spiritual life. He said to me, "Something inside of me died." John spoke for thousands. I could name many myself. Are all lay leaders being bludgeoned? Of course not, but many are.

This administrative culture is draining the life out of institutional churches. Members are considered either supporters or opponents of the pastor and his programs. The locus of power rests in the church business meeting where members either support or oppose the direction of ministry. The pastor becomes a political candidate. His life is public. He is fair game for critical barbs from the loyal opposition. The church environment becomes a world of petitions, caucuses, and interest groups. Every group wants to be represented on the board, and power is won by votes or filibustering change.

Many church members desire to be part of something in which their voices count and their efforts make a difference. Yet, they feel powerless. If a church esteems administrative leadership, the followers will gravitate toward the same values. This is what happens when people are trained to think of power in the church as political in nature. Church leadership should be ministerial rather than political.

Maintainers Rather Than Leaders

The maintainer as a leader has done us great damage. The manager/maintainer is the inevitable result of the institutional church environment. When a church produces executives rather than disciples and politicians rather than ministers, then it will be led by maintainers rather than leaders.

Managers follow leaders like form follows function. When managers lead, few follow. No one needs to follow because managers maintain the status quo; they are gifted at keeping things the way they are. Take the example of a group of managers cutting their way through a jungle. They plot the path, use the best machetes and the proper techniques. A leader comes along and climbs a tree. After viewing the larger landscape, he calls down to the managers, "Wrong Jungle!" [2]

Managers want to improve what is. The form must dictate the function. Managers pray for revival, yet God must revive according to their schedule and work through their forms. Hey, God, they proclaim. We pray from 7:00 to 8:00 on Wednesday evenings in the chapel. Be there! Managers limit God's ability to work because of their comfortable forms. The church needs managers in leadership teams, but it does not need them as the prime leaders.

Programmers Rather Than Philosophers

Programmic thinking has generated as much pain for the church as any external factor. A typical example is the new pastor who wants to replace the Wednesday evening prayer meeting in the chapel with Bible studies in homes. He reasons that, instead of ten people praying in the chapel, nearly one hundred adults will be engaged in prayer in small groups. The philosophical agree, understanding that the issue is function and the function is to pray. They want the change. But the programmic do not agree, and they fiercely attack the proposal. The resulting turmoil leads to special meetings (some consistent with the constitution and bylaws, some not). Threats are made, plans are devised, petitions are circulated. Fear and anger saturate the air. The battle is on. In many cases, it goes on for years. Bitterness takes root. People leave the church. Those who stay are wounded and disillusioned. The church loses its mission and becomes a monument to the sins of the flesh. Why does this happen? The church failed to teach the people the difference between method and principle, form and function, program and philosophy.

As we discussed in Part 2, about 80 percent of the population is programmic in its approach to life. These people ask "how" before they ask "why." They understand something's value by how it works. They care about the meaning behind an action, but they do not think about it much. If the programmic were considering a new evangelistic thrust, they would reproduce an already proven program. If the program worked well for a period of time, they would oppose change. Even if the program became ineffective, they would fight to the death for it. Programmic people emphasize the form of ministry, without considering the function.

The difficult task in church disagreement is to convince people to focus on the Christ-commanded function rather than the form. When people are taught the philosophy and scriptural principles behind forms, they stand on common ground. From that point, the merits of various methods can be argued. A leader's task is to teach the congregation the difference between form and function and to give them a principled place to stand. I strongly encourage all leaders to lead their people to fall in love with function, not forms. This is the only way to sustain a relevant church over the years.

The principled church continually changes direction as its crew constantly adjusts the sails to take advantage of the winds. Like a sailing vessel, such a church depends on the prevailing cultural winds to empower its methods. Its sails must be properly set. When the cultural winds change in a programmic church, the ship no longer speeds through the water; it finds itself struggling. An argument ensues on how the sails should be set. The programmic maintain, We have sailed with the sails set this way for the entire trip, and it has worked fine. The more principled respond, The winds have changed; we won't get anywhere like this. The argument goes on. While a decision is being made, the sails are taken down, and the ship either sits in the doldrums or is flailed about.

Leadership Styles

Before continuing, let us digress for a moment and explore the origins of leadership styles. In his book *Effective Church Leadership*, Kennon Callahan offers four leadership styles based on four world views.[3] His critique is germane to the reason church leaders have become the greatest barrier to renewal, and it offers a cultural exposé on leadership origins.

Life is material, leadership is management. Therefore, leadership is the management of that material. This type of leader focuses on the functional, economic well-being of the organization. The bottom-line issue is dollars and attendance. This person treats the church like a business. God's will is determined by the projected income, based on economic research and market trends. The sign of a good church is a growing, well-monitored budget that stays in the black. This type of leadership breeds an institutional mindset with a theology of survival, maintenance, and scarcity.

Life is a hierarchy, leadership is being a boss. This is the type of leader who gains and uses power. The more power (and control), the better. This particular model is rooted in the "top-down," authoritarian culture of the first half of this century. Although it is slipping away, this leadership style is still strong in those conservative churches normally lagging behind culture by twenty years. This philosophy of leadership tends to build a strong caste system. It leads to autocratic leadership with a supporting cast of ministry peons to do the "dirty" work. This is revealed in everything from a theology of parking to the pastor's private bathroom. This style of leadership also widens the clergy/laity gap.

Life is a crisis, leadership is being a charismatic inspirer. This model creates the type of leader who hears from God and then tells the people what God told him. This leadership style creates a generation of spiritually dependent weaklings living from crisis to crisis. They have been trained to wait for their leader to tell them what is important and what they should do next. God tells the charismatic leaders secrets the followers can share only when they follow the leader. Contemporary leaders and followers must learn to avoid this style like the plague.

Life is a process, leadership is being an enabler. This philosophy of leadership sees life in developmental stages. The leader focuses on enabling people through the growing process. Jesus modeled this particular philosophy of leadership. He led twelve disciples through a sequential, segmented training process.[4] It represents the most culturally sensitive leadership style relevant to the needs of modern man.

As Callahan states, "A philosophy of developmentalism rejects the materialism of the world."[5] The real world is the spirit world. It is no better or worse than the material world, but it is just as real. This is exactly the point. This type of leader wants to move people in constructive ways through each stage of their spiritual pilgrimage.

Good leadership is proactive, intentional, and missional.

7

Transformation

I have coined the term "metaLeaders" to describe the leaders who have experienced transformation. (This is based on the Greek word *metanoia,* translated "repentance." To change one's mind is the core of repentance or transformation.) Developing meta-Leaders is to transform, or change, the existing leaders of local churches. It is a vital mission. It is the toughest problem in the institutional church, and it is the most crucial mission of the church to the church. Without metaLeaders, church renewal is surreal.

Developing metaLeadership requires iron wills on the part of its proponents. It will not happen without prayer, well-crafted strategy, and pain. There is no way to accomplish the goal without leaving blood on the floor. There will be casualties on the part of the unwilling, the disobedient, and the entrenched. There will also be serious losses on the part of the transformers. Some resistant leaders will need to be terminated as leaders, and some will transfer to other churches.

The philosophy of the institutional church thinks of God as relating to the world through the church. The leaders view their primary mission as the stability and well-being of the church itself. They want to take care of their own. When they have their house in order, they can go into the world. By contrast, metaLeaders think of God as relating to the world through people (specifically Christians) rather than through the church structure. Since God is already at work in the world, when the church goes into the world, it gets in on what God is doing. The metaLeader will lead a mission church, which believes that the mission must come first. A church's needs are met through self-denial and service to the mission. Only by putting the mission first can the church be the church. Such a church lives by mission like fire lives by oxygen.

Rarely does the institutionalized congregation stay true to its original mission. It abandons the mission in order to serve itself. God does not forsake the world by waiting for the church to act. He shook the very first church in Jerusalem out of its timidity when he brought persecution and scattered them abroad. Naturally they evangelized. God is intentional, caring, and determined to reach the world. When a church agrees and gets on board, its people are tracking with God.

The metaLeader's first concern is for people, inside and outside the church. His focus is mission, not maintenance, service, or survival. His greatest fear is implosion, that the church will collapse under the weight of its own selfishness.

Jesus said, "If anyone would come after me, he must deny himself and take up his cross daily and follow me. For whoever wants to save his life will lose it, but whoever loses his life for me will save it" (Luke 9:23–24). The irony is that, if we attempt to save our lives, not only will the mission die but the person will die as well. Any Christian who forsakes the call to mission will die a little each day, knowing he is walking in disobedience. Survival of self or institution as the mission is spiritual suicide.

How do we transform existing leaders? The answer is five-fold. We must establish redemptive relationships. We must study. We must develop a commitment to the new vision. We must deal directly with detractors. And finally, we must institutionalize the vision.

Establish Redemptive Relationships

To redeem means to pay a price. A redemptive relationship is one in which the members have paid a price. They have invested time, emotion, and money into each other. Such a relationship is open and honest, built on trust and mutual respect. This sharply contrasts with the relationships maintained by many church leaders that are superficial, formal, and suspicious. How many times have you heard the following story? On returning from vacation, the pastor finds a letter on his desk requesting his resignation. On Friday afternoon, two elders unexpectedly call on him and inform him he should resign. Without the knowledge of the pastor, the church board has been holding meetings and listening to congregational complaints. Board members have written letters to denominational leaders, complaining about the pastor. Members have written letters and phoned board members detailing their grievances.

On the other side of the coin, the pastor orchestrates plots and vendettas against problem board members. He attempts to rally advocates for his position against the "church boss." Whenever he gets the opportunity, he drops in such spiritual barbs as: "Joe is a dear brother, but he is a traditionalist, and he is in the way of the Lord on this issue"; or, "Don't tell him I said this, but I will oppose his returning to the board." Pastors have even been known to fix nominations by secretly planting seeds of doubt about certain individuals with key decision makers. Often, they think of themselves as warriors for the Lord in a spiritual battle, but the enemy is not Satan, it is Elder Frank and his friends. Or worse, the enemy is an unidentified interest group opposing the pastor's leadership.

The above scenario describes typical leadership that lacks integrity and cannot be supported by Scripture. In fact, to relate this way is a grievous sin. It is particularly sad when spiritual leaders relate by way of surrogates and subterfuge. This is far from redemptive. God desires leaders to model open and honest relationships. This example also illustrates a lack of moral courage and conviction. Leaders hold a responsibility to model right relational values before their congregation.

The challenge is to transform relationships from adversarial to redemptive. How do we do this? By making a commitment to respect God's relational rules, by investing informal time, and by investing in emotional understanding. Let's look at each of these methods separately.

The first one is *to make a commitment to respect God's relational rules.* This is simple, hard, risky, revolutionary, and wonderful. God's rules are straightforward. "Therefore, if you are offering your gift at the altar and there remember that your brother has something against you, leave your gift there in front of the altar. First go and be reconciled to your brother; then come and offer your gift" (Matt. 5:23–24). If you have a difference with a brother, talk to him alone first. This one obedient action among leaders would solve the majority of problems. It would lead to more pristine worship and bring a new level of trust and integrity to relationships.

Another simple rule applies as well. If you think your colleague has sinned, go to him alone and talk to him about it. "If your brother sins against you, go and show him his fault, just between the two of you. If he listens to you, you have won your brother over" (Matt. 18:15). Scripture continues with instructions on bringing in others if the first step does not work. The point here is to demonstrate respect for God and friends by dealing directly and with integrity.

How many times do people opt out of this command by reasoning that the brother will not listen or by thinking the church leadership should know first? Or perhaps they attend "private" meetings with one or two surprise guests. Yet, the biblical command is clear.

We must start somewhere. If church leadership teams desire to please God and impact their followers, they must start with the principle of respecting God's relational rules.

The second method for transforming adversarial relationships is *to invest informal time.* Someone once said, "If the man in me likes the man in you, we can be friends. We can work together. But if the little boy in me likes the little boy in you, we can be soul mates. We can trust each other." I have spoken with many church leaders who claimed they could never tell their colleagues what they were feeling. They feared that the others would talk, and this knowledge about them would change what the people thought. Part of the reason for this is that men rarely take the time to bond with one another, and since most of our church leaders are men, this greatly affects the church.

An effective way to truly reach a deeper trust level is through informal play. The redemptive relationship begins when we decide that others are worth a commitment of my time at play. Once we begin to spend informal playtime together, we start thinking about each other as human beings and fellow laborers, not as critics of our weaknesses.

The third way to transform adversarial relationships into redemptive relationships is *to invest in emotional understanding.*

Three specific illustrations demonstrate the meaningful progress leading toward integrity when leaders take the time to understand each other's emotional needs. On one particular occasion, a fellow leader had been complaining about a ministry assignment. Some thought he had "lost it" spiritually. One evening on a retreat, he revealed the source of his frustration in the middle of an emotionally charged discussion. This broke the issue open and led to a new freedom for him to minister. On another occasion, a man was able to talk about his struggles with his father. This man needed the approval of others. He looked to the approval of surrogate fathers in the congregation. This made it hard for him to be decisive and stand firm on his convictions. A third leader was able to admit his reasons for sympathizing with a particular group in his church. He had opposed the pastor's leadership because his friends did. Even though he had disagreed with them, he had not wanted to lose his friends. His friends had meant more to him than the principle.

One good way to understand what makes fellow leaders tick is personality testing. There are a number of such tests that measure basic temperament and workstyle preference. Some of my most meaningful, team-building experiences have been built around this simple assessment tool. It has helped us understand what motivates one another and why we view each other in certain ways. It has also helped us rearrange our assigned work to everyone's advantage. When we understand each other, we have greater empathy. When we feel with others, we share their emotional life. This bonds people together and causes them to support one another. It encourages loyalty and can transform church leadership relationships from adversarial to redemptive.

Stay Close to Your Enemies

To establish redemptive relationships, a leader must act with integrity with respect to his opponents. This is done by staying close to one's opponents. Never surprise them. Talk to them. Spend time with them. Be honest and direct. Follow Jesus' advice. "But I tell you who hear me: Love your enemies, do good to those who hate you, bless those who curse you, pray for those who mistreat you" (Luke 6:27). What a strategy! Think of nice things you can do for your enemies. Pray for them. Pray that God will bless them. Although this is expensive emotionally because it risks rejection, it brings true redemption. Jesus tells us the way to win our enemies is through love, directness, honesty, and integrity. Few enemies will be able to resist such a barrage. This process costs plenty—that's why it is called redemptive. When you give yourself to others, you will get hurt. When you lay your heart down before others, someone will surely stomp on it. But the risk is worth it. The pain is worth it. It brings redemption.

Redemptive relationships build emotional equity that can save the church from self-destruction during serious conflict. When difficulty comes, and it will come, a church's survival depends on the amount of emotional equity built up among the leaders. Trust, loyalty, and a belief in the integrity of fellow leaders build a foundation of emotional equity. The task of renewal must be supported through redemptive relationships built on such equity.

Study

The second principle for transforming existing leaders is to study with them. There is no way to sustain a movement on emotion. Since the power of ideas is clearly superior to the power of emotion, emotional energy must be connected to intellectual energy. Three of the most charismatic figures of our century, Mao, Stalin, and Hitler, had the ability to excite people with the spoken word, but their greatest strength was found in their ideas: Stalin had communism; Hitler had fascism: and Mao had the "Little Red Book." What does a pastor have? He has the most powerful idea known to man, Christianity.

If renewal in leadership is going to take place, leaders must rally around something in which they believe. That starting point is, of course, the Bible. Once a pastor has reached his people's hearts through a redemptive relationship, he must reach their hearts with God's ideas and mission. He must call his leaders to study and learn with him. This way, he will achieve unity.

Unity is based on principles rather than relationships. Unity is supported by relationships, but relationships are not a sufficient basis for it. Principles and concepts, such as a doctrinal position, a specialized mission, or a common concern, form a solid base for unity that can be experienced by people who attend the same church but do not know each other.

The first church had 3,000 members the first day. This number swelled to 5,000, then to 10,000. The church still had unity (Acts 2:44; 4:32). Contemporary churches of 5,000 or more are now experiencing great unity. To achieve it, the pastor must teach his leaders to walk toward a theology of mission. They must study and learn together. The key to change is the mind. "Do not conform any longer to the pattern of this world, but be transformed by the renewing of your mind" (Rom. 12:2). A person can be moved emotionally and make resulting changes. Because of the relationship stimulus brought about through redemption, a person may try to behave differently or accommodate a friend's wishes. However, such change is only temporary. There is no substitute for the supernatural transformation taking place when the Holy Spirit, joined with Scripture, implants God's thoughts into a willing mind. The secret to sustaining a lifetime change and commitment to Jesus Christ is a scripturally based belief system.

The pastor is the philosophic architect of his church. He cannot delegate the task of creating the mission. In *The Strategies for Taking Charge*, Warren Bennis studied ninety chief executive officers. He discovered the most amazing facts. "In no case did one of our effective leaders delegate the task of shaping social architecture to anyone else. Nor did we find one effective leader whose activities, when it comes to influencing the social architecture, ever run down or abate."[6] Bennis concluded that all ninety leaders had the ability to translate intention into reality, and to sustain it.

Bob Singleton, an experienced disciple-maker who devoted seven years toward building a ministry in one church, wrote, "This movement of discipleship and evangelism CANNOT be maintained unless it is initially built by the PASTOR. . . . The vision, energy and time to see the movement develop must, I believe, be channeled from the Lord through him from the beginning and throughout the life of the movement."[7]

Bennis and Singleton agree. Leaders cannot delegate such a vital task. The pastoral leader begins with a new and compelling vision. Then he lifts his mission statement from the pages of Scripture and presents it to the congregation. The pastor who thinks he can continue to preach sermons, while leaving strategy and vision to others, is setting himself up for a fall.

Now, let us move to some practical steps for helping others study the nature of the church and church leadership. Invite the leadership first. While it is not necessary that they all come, it is necessary they all clearly receive an invitation. Invite any unofficial leaders or potential leaders. Make it clear you will be studying the nature of the church and church leadership. Schedule the meetings for a convenient time and date. Provide workbooks, books, and other aids to make the study more interesting. Offer a short break of two or three weeks after each study cycle. Then, start again on the next logical phase.

The purpose is not to win every leader. The purpose is to identify those who grasp the concepts and want to adopt them. Before long, those who are not interested will drop out and thereby lose ground on which to oppose the pastor later. The favoritism issue is also diffused because the participants willingly eliminated themselves from the process. (Those who oppose the pastor's study and direction after this usually have a different agenda. At that point, the question is one of power—who is in charge—and this must be handled in a separate, and quite different, forum.)

This study phase should last one year to eighteen months. During this time, several things should happen. First, several kindred spirits should arise, those for whom the "lights go on." These will be the true believers, those whose hearts burn with excitement as they get a taste of what the church can be. Be sure to get together with these people on an individual basis. Answer their questions and listen to their dreams. Tell them your dreams and keep casting the vision.

Second, opportunities to compare and contrast church practice with scriptural truth should come up. Look for them. For example, the Bible commonly places more emphasis on leader qualifications than the church does. Scripture also describes the role of elders as ministerial, contrasting with the largely administrative role given to elders in most churches today.

This long-term study should have a built-in, self-discovery instrument, calling for weekly assignments to require group members to think through the material. (One such instrument is found in the study guide appendix to my book, *Jesus Christ, Disciple Maker.*) As members go through the process of self-discovery, they develop stronger ownership of what they've learned. They become true believers, and they become the pastor's advocates.

The objective for them is to discover what the pastor already sees. (I would suggest consulting either the workbook for *The Disciple-Making Pastor* or the appendix in *Jesus Christ, Disciple Maker* for guidelines, including questions to facilitate a theology of mission.) If the pastor's view is scripturally sound, the leaders will see it, too. If he leads them to the right texts, they will catch the vision. A leader visualizes the future. By using the Word, the students can see the same image and move toward it with the pastor. As their final work product, the group should write a theology of mission.

The next step is to make the mission a possibility.

Develop a Commitment to the New Vision

Too many study groups collapse under the weight of their own unused knowledge. They file their reports but nothing is done. Knowledge without application is like insight into pathology without a proposed therapy. Many church leaders have been trained as executive policy makers. They are not accustomed to applying their decisions or participating in the results of their policies. But the commitment to the vision and a crafted theology of mission will move these leaders out of their comfort zones.

Learning requires two processes. The first is study, or assimilation of the content. The second is application, or the actual practice of the content. When the United States Army studied learning patterns, it found that if a person would listen, view, and write down what he was told, he could retain up to 50 percent of the material. However, if the learner would add one related, practical activity to the hearing, seeing, and writing, the retention level would jump to 95 percent. This confirms what we already know: theory plus practice is the key to effective learning.

Christ invited the twelve to "come and be with me" (Mark 3:13–14). Why? In order "that they might be with him"—the emphasis was relationship; and, in order "that he might send them out to preach"—the emphasis was mission (Mark 3:14). In order for a conviction about the studied vision to be realized, a personal commitment to the mission is absolutely necessary.

The process of developing commitment to the vision and a crafted theology of mission is three-fold. We must select, train, and manage.

Selection

In my three pastorates, I selected a few from the many. In my larger traditional church, I observed the behavior of leaders and asked scores of parishioners for advice about good small group leaders. I considered people with hearts on fire. If a person had stayed with the study group, if he or she had risen to the surface by faithful attendance and assignments and good communication skills, I considered that person equipped in aptitude for group leadership. I considered the person's standing in the congregational mind as well. Most importantly, I made sure each selectee grasped and agreed with the disciplemaking concepts.

In my smaller established congregation, I worked with existing small group leaders who had already demonstrated an ability and willingness to learn. I looked for the teachable, available person. I sought those who were comfortable with evangelism, knowing that without personal witness as part of their portfolio, the leader would lack integrity.

In the church planting context, I started with a generic study group generated by a congregational invitation. The church that is planted offers a level playing field. In such a situation, official leaders have not yet been identified or selected, and the process has not been poisoned by preconceived notions. After ten weeks, I chose two men and met separately with them on a weekly basis. I challenged them to watch me work for the next ten weeks. After that time frame, I allowed each to lead a group as I managed their work.

Select twice as many leaders as you will need. If you want to start three groups of ten in one year, and have a family church setting, then select six couples. If some drop out of the training process, you will still have a minimum of one couple to lead each group. If everyone stays, you can send them out in teams of two couples each, choosing one couple as the leaders and the other as apprentices. (I must add that I have never known a successful group led by a married man whose wife did not attend and give her full support.) If the church has a configuration other than family, select appropriately.

In Matthew 4:19, Jesus said, "Follow me and I will make you [to become] fishers of men." Here, the Lord gave us a model for the invitation. "Follow me" implies a new, close relationship. "I will make you to become" communicates responsibility for training and growth.

"Fishers of men" is a contextualized vision statement to make the follower someone special, a fisher of men. This invitation has all the necessary ingredients for giving followers the confidence, comfort, and vision they need. If a leader wants people to drop their briefcases, computer keyboards, and real estate contracts, his selection must combine commonsense selectivity with vision.

Many pastors tell me their people will not commit. Yet people do commit if they are adequately prepared before they are challenged.[8] People will also commit if they are properly challenged. They need the truth about the cost. They also need an outline of the benefits as well as the vision. The vision is vitally important, for this is what pulls people toward extraordinary commitment and sacrifice. I have seen this happen hundreds of times.

One way people try to slip out of commitment is to maintain that they didn't know such and such would happen. I liken commitment to marriage. When I promised to have and to hold, there was a great deal I did not know. There was a great deal my wife did not know. Yet, despite some difficult days, we haven't excused ourselves from our commitment simply because of a lack of clairvoyance. Christians should be committed to the Lord. Consequently, I often ask whether God knew what was going to happen when he led the person to make the commitment. The answer is obvious: he did. Therefore, the person should continue to trust that God will lead him with all the information at his call.

Training

No more effective training option exists than piloting the leaders through the group model. Here, the first order of business is to develop, or choose, the model. A model includes the group's mission, and it permits the group to answer the following questions: Is the group opened or closed? What material will it use? What will be the commitment level? How long will it meet? Much more will be said about small-group theory later. For now, the point is to ask and answer these questions. (I do not advocate allowing input before you have your basic principles together. The only exception might be when the alpha leaders—or first generation of leaders—are philosophically on your team.)

Let's say the basic disciplemaking group you want to model has a two-year cycle, and you need to compress this time period into nine to twelve months. The same type of Bible study can be done with only a portion covered. Since your alpha group lacks the advantage of repeated experience, it is crucial not to leave out any relevant experience. For example, if the group is built around Bible study, community, prayer, and outreach, it should focus on repeating these basic disciplines as much as possible.

After nine to twelve months, your potential leaders should surface. At this juncture, the challenge is to select group leaders and assign the remaining members as apprentices. Follow basic relational rules in explaining your decisions and then match the right apprentices with the leaders. You can do this based on such areas as friendships, giftedness, desire, and availability. Next, help them form groups. Very few will be able to establish groups without assistance. As novice leaders, they will find it difficult to talk about group covenant or rules and discuss accountability issues with friends. When their friends challenge the ideas, they will not be able to defend the covenant.

I would suggest a formal orientation for all interested in joining a group. This should be announced from the pulpit, supported by the pastor, and placed in church literature. The meeting should be led by the pilot group leader. It should clearly present the reasons for such groups, the benefits of joining, and the cost of commitment. Potential group members should be given one week to make their final decision. (It is advisable, however, to secure as many decisions at the meeting as possible.) Those who have already decided can be placed into groups that evening. Commitment cards are taken by the pilot group leader and new group leaders.

The groups are usually 50 percent full following the orientation. After about a week the group leaders call those who are undecided. These are assigned to groups as well, although this is not finalized until they agree. While the wishes of group members as to their assignment is honored whenever possible, the final decision lies with the small-group director.

Management

The third step is management. This means guiding the leaders through a two-year process of leading their own groups.[9] Leading small groups that are task-oriented is the very best training ground for leaders. Hands-on leadership experience is the optimum environment for developing such skills as creating vision, sticking to the mission, leading people, correcting the wayward, disciplining the rebellious, providing support and intimacy, reaching the unreached, administering tasks, teaching Scripture, and facilitating the learning of Scripture.

A leader who is willing to take responsibility for his own actions and decisions is a rare leader indeed. In too many leadership contexts, apprentices and trainers kick the heat upstairs, avoiding tough issues when they are challenged. This is a vital leadership training issue. The group leader must defend himself and take the heat as well. That is part of leadership. If a person cannot, or will not, take full responsibility for his group's philosophy and requirements, he will fail. A person who folds at this level will also collapse as a church leader. Beware of leaders who cannot take the relationship heat. Do not let them lead!

The management phase of leadership development can be accomplished through the formal leadership community, or in a less formal way. The important issue is that the leaders are managed, helped, and coached through their training experience. The most often repeated mistake in leadership development is that potential leaders are not taught while on the job or held accountable for their actions. They are not well-trained. They go their own way. They do not respect spiritual authority. If quality control is to be developed in a church leadership team, it must be developed during this crucial stage.

Deal with Detractors

The process of training leaders can revolutionize leadership. The transformed lives and changed values will spur the leaders toward giving themselves fully to the Great Commission. The majority will be captivated by the vision and motivated to service for the kingdom. A minority, however, will resist the prevailing winds of change. After a grace period of unpredictable length, detractors will inevitably oppose the new ideas. This opposition will not be based on their ideology. These battles are almost always over who is in charge—they are power struggles. Regardless of the amount of religious language employed, the issue is power. Not all detractors will actively oppose the new realities. Some, who do not like the new environment but do not want to cause trouble, will quietly slip into the background. Their detraction is by failure to support the new leadership. A second set exists, however, and this one can be quite dangerous. These people have position, history, and spheres of influence. If they simply drop negative comments here and there without an attempt to mobilize, they can be tolerated. But if they actively seek to discredit and bring down the leadership, they must be handled swiftly. Such active detractors are masters of misdirection and numerous avoidance techniques. Catching one is like a cat trying to catch a bird. You see it, you know what it is doing, and just when you think you have it, it flies away.

Detractors do not expect to pay for their slander, gossip, and destruction of group unity and morale. They do not openly oppose. Most of their behavior is subterfuge. When confronted, few will "fess up." They would rather spend years building up bad feelings than be proven wrong. They function best in an ambiguous environment where they can hide behind rules and regulations, policies and procedures. They feel helpless and naked when confronted one-on-one with a Bible.

The arsenal of these detractors includes slander, gossip, innuendo, cynicism, and other baser weapons. They act threatened, hurt, bitter, and sanctimonious. These people cloak their bitterness and anger in religious language. Satan almost always attacks by use of the naive and the bitter, and by use of "god talk" to deceive those innocent ones who can be swayed one direction or the other. Phrases used by such well-intentioned Satanic conduits include: "This is an unfortunate situation"; "I must regrettably report to you . . . "; "I've been in this church for thirty-six years now, and I've never seen such autocratic leadership." Translated, what these statements really mean is that the person has never been challenged as "church boss" before or felt so powerless.

My word to you is to deal directly and firmly with such opposition. The older I get, the more I believe God will honor his relational principles, such as Matthew 18:15–18 and Matthew 5:23–24. As much as

I dislike confrontation, the alternative is worse. Living with the results of disobedience to God's direction is harder.

The author of Proverbs warns us about the devastation of the unchecked tongue.

> There are six things the LORD hates,
> seven that are detestable to him:
> haughty eyes,
> a lying tongue,
> hands that shed innocent blood,
> a heart that devises wicked schemes,
> feet that are quick to rush into evil,
> a false witness who pours out lies
> and a man who stirs up dissension
> among brothers.
>
> [Prov. 6:16–19]

The devil has used many good people to do what God despises. Many well-intentioned members commit the above sins in order to "save" their church. This is a battle! You are fighting an enemy who desires to destroy you, an enemy who takes prisoners. Like a thief, he wants to rob you. Like a murderer, he wants to kill you. He is a pathological liar. He does not play fair, and he does not care who gets hurt. Therefore, expect bloody warfare in the church when bitter, hostile disciples become the devil's tools.

For too long the weapons of our warfare have not been spiritual. They have been secular and political. The church has fought the wrong enemy. The fight has been intramural, with the wrong tools and the wrong enemy. The weapons of our warfare are divinely powerful and can knock down strongholds and take every thought or ideology captive to the obedience of Christ. Our enemy is Satan and his legions. Our weapons are supernatural. Political power is earthly, fleshly, and inadequate. Spiritual power is heavenly, spiritual, and more than adequate.

We must meet the enemy head-on in the power of the Spirit and defeat him with the power and blood of Christ. Do not back off. If you do, Satan wins, and the church loses. When the devil tries to make the battle personal, do not succumb. Deal directly, firmly, and in love. Set your goal to restore the troublemakers. Transform them by the power of Christ, permit them to transfer to another church, or have them terminate their membership. It is better to deal directly and fight the necessary battle than to let the unresolved hostility continue and eat the heart out of your church.

Institutionalize the Vision

Once the new leaders are trained and old leaders transformed, it is time to bring them together in official capacities. To institutionalize the vision means to bring it to the point of becoming a well-known purpose statement. Just as other ideas and traditions were once the understood values of the church, now the new ideas are. This is the natural result of the transformation of existing leaders.

I am acquainted with several churches that have made this journey. One was a church that mixed seventy elderly members from one dying church with two hundred college students led by a young pastor. The new church grew to over five hundred in a few months. The transition was made with mutual respect between both groups, including unity on a board comprised of representatives from the old and new.

Some pastors are presently in the midst of this dangerous but necessary journey. Some have been deeply wounded. Others have become casualties. But most are going to make it. Church renewal without pain is a fantasy. I am greatly encouraged by the many courageous leaders, both clergy and lay, who are committed to doing right and transforming the church.

Conclusion

Evangelical leadership needs transformation. We have made executives rather than disciples, politicians rather than ministers, maintainers rather than leaders, and programmers rather than philosophers. In order for this transformation to take place, we must establish redemptive relationships, study, develop a commitment to a new vision, deal directly with detractors, and institutionalize the vision. By following this five-fold approach, we will enable church leaders to become spiritually motivated and ministry minded.

Part 4

We Must Cast the Vision

or

It Takes More Than Talk

The pastor can no longer sit in his study pondering the relations of sin to the greatest good, or of foreordination to free will. He must be out among the people with his eye and often his hand on every value and lever of church machinery.

—G. B. Wilcox

8

The Inspirational Vehicle

Preaching is the first and most important step in the disciplemaking process. It stands out, unstained by the soiled fabric of everyday life. It offers the pastor an unfettered opportunity to lead his flock. Doing the best job possible in the pulpit is a priority for any pastor. It makes everything else better and easier. Keeping in mind his overall ministry intention, a pastor should regularly explain biblical values, the mission of the church, and his specific strategy from the pulpit. If a pastor cannot motivate and inspire from the pulpit, he should not be preaching. When a pastor passionately presents the values, the vision, and the strategy for his church in his sermons, then his people will be inspired and mobilized toward the goal. People respond to high commitment tasks when they understand how the pieces fit together and make a difference. Then they will apply what they've learned by doing such things as eliminating committees, joining small groups, and rewriting the constitution. **If pastors are going to lead the church of the twenty-first century, they must begin with their sermons.**

Leading requires the casting of vision: The leader describes the vision with passion and vivid language. He believe it so deeply that his presentation compels his listeners to action. From this, he will be able to gather a small army of loyalists and lead his people through change, without traumatizing the entire church.

Augustine once compared the gifted orator with the common speaker. A particular door had two keys, one golden and the other wooden. The golden key symbolized the gifted orator while the wooden represented the common communicator. Augustine noted that, if the wooden key opened the door and the golden did not, the wooden key was of greater value. Every pastor does not have to be a highly gifted public speaker. A person who can communicate clearly and with conviction can provide inspirational leadership beginning with his sermons.

Let's look at three examples of well-trained, disciplemaking pastors who lost their ministries because of a failure to lead through their sermons. The first is Joe. Joe believed all the right things. He was well-trained; his motives were pure, and his integrity impeccable. He carefully engineered his leaders through the treacherous terrain of new paradigms. As official changes were made, Joe was encouraged, but he failed to paint a picture in his sermons and give people a reason to sacrifice and overcome the discomforts associated with change. Then the unexpected happened. Attendance fell along with giving, and Joe's salary was cut. He resigned under pressure. What went wrong? Joe lacked the ability to inspire.

The second illustration is Robert, an associate pastor. Robert believed the right things and said the right things in his sermons. After a year or so, however, the congregation began to attack Robert on a variety of issues, not one of which touched doctrine or mission. Why? Robert had failed to inspire and motivate the congregation. He had failed to lead them over the next hill in their minds to see new vistas of opportunity. Although he had excellent plans for the church, he could not motivate the congregation to see what he could see. The congregation dismissed him.

Our final example is Frank, who planted a church and worked in a "tentmaking" position until the new congregation could pay his salary. A decade later, church membership totaled more than seven hundred with a staff of five. The church had just completed a major building program when the elders informed Frank he should consider moving on. How could they do this? The reason was simple. The elders had never captured the vision. Frank failed to lead through his sermons.

Although he was a good speaker, his excellent sermons were not of much use because they did not lead the people toward the vision. Unless the pastor provides the vision through the inspirational vehicle of his sermon, unity is lost. During the ten years, Frank had not been able to fuse together a team of men totally committed to a common vision. Frank refused to quit. As a result, the elders walked out, his staff resigned, and more than half the congregation left.

9

The Paradigm Shift

paradigm shift is crucial to saving the evangelical church today. *Paradigm* is derived from the Greek word for "model" or "method" and here means a set of assumptions governing our view of the church and its priorities. We need to shift away from the hermetically sealed pulpit with no real life in it toward the leadership pulpit. Continuation of the pulpit-dependent church will facilitate evangelical irrelevancy and demise. Many small churches in our country are dominated by this model, which defines outreach as bringing people to church to hear the pastor preach and issue an altar call. Such a church cannot rise above the pastor's preaching ability. I believe we can train men to think differently and, therefore, to behave differently with respect to the pulpit ministry. The church must make the shift to multi-dimensional outreach and evangelism.

To think in terms of building a church based on the leadership pulpit with team outreach, leadership development, and relational networks is to reap a tremendous harvest. This is what our seminary students need to learn, but this requires a faculty who understand. Currently, our seminaries are factories producing sermon makers. It is irresponsible for denominations and their seminaries to perpetuate the myth that this is what makes a pastor. Preachers and counselors dominate practical theology departments. We must shift to a focus on leadership and strategy, in addition to preaching. Homileticians could better serve the church by exploring the new paradigms in preaching and by producing leaders who can also preach.

Leadership, rather than preaching, is the most crucial skill in pastoral ministry. A pastor/leader should be trained to:

* teach/preach
* develop a strategy and distill it into a vision statement
* cast vision
* engineer change
* manage people—getting work done through others
* manage conflict

Preaching then becomes one of the many vital skills of a leader. No single person is strong in every area, but everyone must understand the basic skills necessary to his work. This means teaching leaders to view the overall challenge of pastoral work as primarily a function of leadership. From this perspective, a leader will be more inclined to build a group of lay people into a pastoral team. In the long run, this permits the leader to excel in his strengths while the team does the same. In this way, the person thinks along the lines of Ephesians 4:12, "preparing God's people for ministry." Preaching remains vital, but it is no more crucial than other primary skills.

I believe each pastor should press the issues from Scripture and lead. This is not only my opinion, it is my experience. A number of years ago, our church attempted to raise funds for a building project. A particular part of the sermon text I was using lent itself to a strong application regarding financial giving. I applied the text to the existing building project, employing both humor and passion. An offended listener challenged my application. He was bothered by the fact that the sermon had made him and others feel guilty and uncomfortable by cutting so "close to the bone."

Consider how ludicrous this reasoning is: The Scripture is fine until it touches me where I actually live. I agree with those who say preachers should not use the Scripture for personal attack. But the pastor has a responsibility to address the issues. Good preaching must be fused to the real issues a church is facing. Too many people argue, "Just preach the Word. Don't get too specific. Let the Holy Spirit fill in the blanks, and let God do his work. They'll get the picture." I wish this were true, but it isn't. Older evangelicals ask where today's leaders are? Where are the Spurgeons, the Ockengas, the Luthers, and the Lloyd-Jones? The answer is they are gone. They once led effectively, but men like Spurgeon would bomb in today's church. While great preaching in any era always communicates God's truth in a relevant, contextualized manner that moves people to action, looking to the past for answers to the present is folly. Great preaching back then would not necessarily be great preaching today.

Today's new kind of leader is different. He is thoroughly evangelical but has discarded the unnecessary baggage. Although he does not ignore his knowledge of the original languages, he no longer spends hours exegeting the fine points of Greek or Hebrew text. Instead of using his seminary as a means of power, he gleans the relevant and forgets the rest. His preaching is an important part of his leading, but it remains subservient to the overall mission. Today's new leader listens to Garrison Keillor instead of Bob Theime, enjoys Walt Wangerin and quotes Frederick Buechner. He has learned leadership principles from Tom Peters, Steven Covey, and Warren Bennis. He reads Toffler, Lasch, Postman, and Gallup to understand the future. He has learned the power of the story and dabbles in poetry. He views mission as the paramount church issue and realizes his preaching must serve it. He toys with other forms of communication, but is committed to doing what works within scriptural parameters. He does not live an insular life, cloistered away in his study. He spends a good deal of time on the streets, keeping in touch with the marketplace. He works with community networks and starts Bible studies as well as action groups. He plays a major role in crafting vision and developing ministry teams. He is committed to leading the charge.

Today's leader is new, yet in a strange way he is a refreshing throwback to the past. He retains the much needed emphasis on pastoral evangelism while rejecting its abuses. Such a pastor models aggressive evangelism for the purpose of training and outreach. He understands the importance of the various ministries but rejects the idea that the pastor should be a "jack of all trades." He is no longer shackled by counseling every need, attending every committee meeting, or visiting every sick parishioner. His schedule is not cluttered with "administrivia," and he does not fall prey to the tyranny of the urgent. He selects the tasks that will comprise 90 percent of his work load and leaves the remaining 10 percent of his time for the unexpected. Today's leader is also determined to engage the enemy directly through personal evangelism. The battle is over eternal souls, and he recognizes this.

10

Only a Part

Preaching alone does not equip the saints or change lives. While a most important part of ministry, it remains only a part. Many young men, like myself, started our ministries thinking the gourmet sermon would entice people. Ephesians 4:12 says that pastor/teachers should equip the saints for the work of ministry. We prided ourselves in doing our best through our expository sermons. Our seminary educations supported this notion. But we had drawn our conclusions built on a false premise, and they were wrong.

It is not true that great preaching always leads to great churches. Church greatness is determined by a number of factors, such as the kind of team a church is putting onto the field and the kind of truth written on the members' hearts. *Sermons alone cannot change lives.*

So, what can sermons do? Are they still a legitimate ministry? Do they need further action to authenticate their purpose? The answer to these questions is yes. Isaiah 55:11 says, "So is my word that goes out from my mouth: It will not return to me empty, but will accomplish what I desire and achieve the purpose for which I sent it." God qualifies this promise by saying that what "goes out" will "achieve the purpose" for which he sent it. It is possible that an ill-conceived sermon delivered for the self-aggrandizement of the preacher could indeed return void. But this Scripture pronounces blessing on the well-intended presentation of God's Word. If the teacher believes Scripture, is filled with the Holy Spirit, and teaches with integrity, he can claim this promise.

However, verbal presentation of the Scripture is only the beginning of the learning process. Paul exhorted Timothy on the value and primacy of Scripture. "All Scripture is God-breathed and is useful for teaching, rebuking, correction and training in righteousness, so that the man of God may be thoroughly equipped for every good work" (2 Tim. 3:16–17).

No one is trained without the use of Scripture. Leaders are called to "prepare God's people for the work of ministry" (Eph. 4:12). So, the question is not one of priority of Scripture, but rather how Scripture is used in the training of God's people. In this context, teaching applies to presenting the Word, regardless of application.

Romans 12:2 tells us that change starts in the mind with the new data of Scripture as the necessary information. Hebrews 4:12 indicates that the Word penetrates the inner regions of a person's mind. Verbal presentation alone does not create change, but without it, change is impossible. The listener can decide to change. He can be under conviction of God's Spirit and confess his sins, but he must stand up and go out to apply the principles. Real change manifests itself in transformed behavior (Acts 26:20).

The Learning Process

The church cannot get along without these effective verbal presentations of Scripture. The accurate, clear, and practical biblical message is the first and most important step in the learning process, but it represents only the first two of six steps that comprise learning. Let us explore a full, orbicular teaching model.[1]

Steps 1 and 2

Tell them what and tell them why. Telling people things is not training, nor is it equipping them for ministry. Unless more is done, the pastor is disobedient to his calling. These two steps represent what happens in a sermon or Bible presentation. If a pastor stops here he is what I call a "pastor/teller" rather than a "pastor/teacher."

Steps 3 and 4

Show them how and do it with them. These steps are basic to learning. They require the pastor or his team to step out from behind the lectern and model the desired behavior. They call for the leader to create training vehicles, placing teacher and learner together in a learning context. In order for a learner to memorize Scripture, share his faith, explore inductive Bible study, lead a small group, or do basic counseling, he first needs to see these things take place and then do them while being supervised.

Steps 5 and 6

Let them do it and deploy them. In step five, a change takes place. The supervisor is no longer present. The learner reports back, however, on a regular basis for further training and refinement. Step six launches the learner into ongoing ministry leadership without regular supervision. Contact is retained, but is loosely strung, based on already proven performance.

Pastors must not stop with their sermons. They must go on. The sermon should be subject to the larger mission. This means that what is preached, how it is preached, and its applications are determined by the overreaching concerns of fulfilling the Great Commission. Such preaching is connected to steps three through six in the six-step teaching method just discussed. Its application calls for direct involvement in the application vehicles, making these three steps a reality.

The Mission First

The mission must come first. Today's contemporary teacher loves to speak of the mission to reach the world. He enjoys the radical message of discipleship, so clearly taught by Jesus in such passages as Luke 9:23–25. Following Jesus, however, calls for self-denial. It is the prerequisite to taking up our cross or mission in life. By losing ourselves in the mission, Scripture promises we will find ourselves and fulfill our life's purpose.

Self-denial in the pulpit means the pastor becomes a giver; he preaches for results in the hearer's life, not for evaluation of his presentation. In practice, however, many pastors rarely apply this mandate to their preaching. Self-denial in the pulpit is a foreign concept in today's ego-driven society. A seductive and powerful force is at work, which makes servant preaching a supernatural challenge.

The young seminarian is eager and optimistic about his future. When exposed to a "successful" pastor, the student hears the pastor attribute God's blessing to the pulpit. This happens almost without exception. (Try to find a pastor who says preaching is not his dominant gift; one willing to admit such a truth is rare indeed.) The young student quickly learns that good preaching is the road to pastoral success, that it is the stimulus for the homage paid by the seminary community to such leaders. If the students want the same respect, they need to move in the same direction.

The seminary community puts undue emphasis on the sermon, but the local church does it even more. Most search committees do not associate preaching with leadership, but most of the time, the first thing a pulpit committee desires is someone strong in the pulpit. Although there is nothing wrong with wanting interesting sermons, the issue is one of priorities. Far too many church members measure their church by the quality of the sermons. When someone is invited to church, it is to hear the pastor. Following his sermon, the pastor retreats to the back door to receive his weekly evaluation from the congregation. Many times a pastor determines his self-worth by what is said at the door.

Pastors are normal human beings with regular emotional needs. If taught that the sermon is paramount, then it is only natural for them to evaluate their ministry through how well they perform. If honor and praise go to the best speakers, then such pastors will strive to be the best speakers. While there is nothing wrong with excellence, there is something wrong when it is confined to a sermon. When a man preaches well, all else seems to be forgiven. He is not held accountable for the broader pastoral task of truly training the saints.

When a sermon becomes the vehicle for the way-I-meet-my-ego-needs-and-earn-self-respect, I am preaching to get a good response. I want to make the congregation enjoy it. I want to entertain them. I want them to think I am a great speaker. I want to offer a gourmet's delight, letting the words roll off my lips and into their spirits in such a way that it tastes good. I do not want to anger them or make them feel guilty or teach distasteful things and make them squirm. I want to please them. This, my friends, is the way to corrupt the pulpit. (I know because I have done it enough to be an expert.) To use the sermon to meet my own ego needs and feed my lust is selfish and wrong. Yet it is widely practiced. The evangelical community has made an idol out of pulpits and the men who fill them. It is tragic that we have idolized what was meant only to be a part of the pastoral task. The sermon should serve, not dictate. It should bring homage to God and dedication to his mission. It should be the beginning of a larger strategy for making the church great, not the lone measure of a church. It should be one of the things a pastor does well, not his source of self-esteem.

The selection of biblical texts in a pastor's sermon should relate to the current needs of the church. Some may argue that the biblical text should dictate the message and its applications; otherwise, we have corrupted the holiness and high calling of preaching. I would agree if I thought mission-serving preaching would corrupt the integrity of the biblical text. I am not suggesting that the text be twisted. Rather, I am advocating that the applications connect to the larger mission.

The pastor should develop various series of sermons addressing both strategy and programming. If the church needs small groups, then speak on the biblical basis for small groups. Talk about the characteristics of a faithful disciple. Relate to the people how this can be accomplished through the small group environment. Speak about the small groups in your church and tell them why they should consider involvement. Exhort them to join and tell them where the orientation meeting will be held. If major changes in church structure need to take place in order to be more effective in evangelism, give a series of lectures on why God values outreach. Contrast God's values with existing church practices. Explain the specific structures impeding such outreach. Propose new ways for releasing people toward more effective ministry.

Before preaching can serve the mission, the preacher must be willing to serve the mission. This means that preaching will have radical application and sermons can be applied to real situations. It means talking strategy and telling stories about heroes practicing the right values. It means maximizing sermon length and style to impact people. Being willing to serve the mission means using illustrations from contemporary life, not just from biblical stories. It means spending less time on history, geography, and linguistic analysis and more on what the text means. As Haddon Robinson stated, "Give as much information as the people need to understand the passage and no more. Then move on to application." [2]

In some cases, the church will grow because of excellent sermons. Great preaching does not lead to great churches, however. Church development is not limited to the preaching ability of the pastor. This myth must be corrected. Great churches begin with effective sermons, which serve the greater mission and support the strategy to accomplish that mission.

Meeting the Needs

The measure of a pastor's preaching is the difference his preaching makes in the long run. The measure of a pastor's overall work is what kind of team he puts on the field and whether he stimulates people to action. Is the sermon followed up by practical vehicles to make the desired value a reality? Are people catching a vision for the world, themselves, their community, and their church? Is the pastor giving the congregation a worldview to help them see where they fit and how they could contribute? Finally, is there substantive behavioral change as a result of his total teaching?

Every congregation has two sets of needs that a sermon can meet. The first set is the foundation for all other pulpit work. It is the congregation's need for mission, the vision for the mission, and its scriptural basis. Early in his pastorate, the preacher should present a vision for mission rooted in Scripture. (If he cannot find his vision there, he needs another vision.) A series clearly defining the role of the pastor and people should be offered, with a picture of the finished product and what the church will look like, and be doing, in a decade.

The second set of needs is the specific strengths, weaknesses, conflicts, and crises a particular church faces. The personality of a church determines what is addressed. The reason I mention this is the propensity of pastors to get stuck in "expository ruts." Charles Spurgeon said it well, "I know a minister whose shoe I am unworthy to unloose, whose preaching is often little better than sacred miniature painting—I might almost say holy trifling. He is great upon the ten toes of the beast, the four faces of the cherubim, the mystical meanings of the badger's skins, and the typical bearings of the staves of the ark and the windows of Solomon's temple; but the sins of the businessman, the temptations of the times, and the needs of the age, he scarcely ever touches upon. Such preaching reminds me of a lion engaged in mouse hunting."[3]

Why hunt mice when God has called us to go for the big game? Head toward prevalent sins of the times and, "the needs of the age," as Spurgeon put it. To address a problem when it is real is the most penetrating preaching of all. Do not shrink back from the leading of the Holy Spirit because someone advised you that such teaching makes people squirm, get angry, and attack the preacher. Avoidance of the real issues is for cowards, not responsible pastors.

Martin Luther once said, "The office of preaching is an arduous task. I have often said that if I could come down with a good conscience, I would rather be stretched upon a wheel and carry stones than preach one sermon. For anyone who is in this office will always be plagued; and therefore I have often said that the damned devil and not a good man should be a preacher. But we're stuck with it now. . . . If I had known I would not have let myself be drawn into it with twenty-four horses."[4]

Luther was right. The task of responsible preaching requires the best of a man and often brings out the worst in a congregation. In the long run, however, God honors such integrity with the peaceful fruit of righteousness.

The Second Pulpit

Many pastors know nothing about their other pulpit and, for that reason, do not have one. The absence of a pastor's second pulpit explains the lack of cohesion in his church. What is this pulpit? It is the pastor's ministry to his leaders. Leadership must be nourished and challenged through vision from the heart of the leader. Intentional leadership development is not a strength in the American church. Regardless of polity, optimum human dynamics demand a leader who communicates organizational values and strategy. His "vision casting," the constant stream of stories and impassioned exhortations, will keep the dream alive among the church leaders.

To enhance this second pulpit, a pastor must meet three prerequisites: (1) he must possess a clear vision, based on scriptural values; (2) he must create a leadership forum for nourishing leaders and helping them manage their work; and (3) he must implement an apprenticeship system that allows only the tested and trained to enter the leadership forum. My book, *The Disciple-Making Church*, offers suggestions for creating a leadership community or forum, based on the Pauline model at Ephesus, described in Acts 19:10–18. Such a system nourishes the leader's spirit, produces training grounded in the ministry assignment, and provides encouragement as well as accountability.

The best teams build their overall strategy on the game plan. Once the game begins, the huddle adapts the game plan to the game conditions, and audibles are called at the line of scrimmage to counter specific opposition moves. A church leadership team should have an overall game plan built on scriptural values. The regular leadership forum meets as a huddle to adapt the plan to game conditions. When special opportunities present themselves or the opposition makes an unexpected move, the pastor "calls an audible." If the goal is to advance the ball for the Kingdom of God, even a good punt can gain yardage.

The pastor begins his leadership forum meetings with teaching and vision. The kind of information shared can be sensitive since the meeting is for leaders only. The pastor can also talk in technical terms about specific training principles and techniques. During the second part of the meeting, the various ministry groups huddle for detailed management of their work. Usually, these groups meet twice a month. They work well when led by a senior pastor.

Conclusion

Pastors must begin to lead through their sermons. The sermon is the one thing they do that touches everyone. If pastors will connect their preaching to their philosophy and program, they will foster unity and a visionary congregation more willing to work together. Pastors today must discard the hermetically sealed pulpit and commit themselves to a full, orbicular ministry style in which the mission comes first. Where the sermon serves the mission as well as the pulpit, success is determined by long-term results rather than by the finicky pallet of the contemporary evangelical consumer.

Part **5**

We Must Sacrifice the Forms for the Function

or

Form Must Follow Function

11

Traditions

nd why do you break the command of God for the sake of your tradition?" (Matt. 15:3). Today, Jesus' words cut deeply into the heart of the church just as they did into Pharisaic Judaism. Many churches are immersed in corporate sin because they refuse to change the administrative structures blocking obedience to the Great Commission. Tradition becomes sin when it gets in the way of obedience to Christ. Heritage is great until it creates practical heresy.

We must be willing to deny ourselves the comforts of familiarity for the cause of Christ (Luke 9:23–25). Yet, very few churchmen consider self-denial and taking up one's cross as a mandate to change. For the church to be renewed, it must change. And this change must be administrative.

Twenty-five years ago, it took twenty years for a church methodology to move from inception to irrelevancy. Ten years ago, it was fifteen. Today, the cycle has collapsed to seven years. Because culture is speeding down the road at a frightening pace, leaders today must be willing to live with constant change.

"Some of the toughest problems we face are those created by successes of the past."[1] These words are carried out daily in stalled-out and dying churches. Form leads function along the road to irrelevancy as Satan hands out the directions. In order to remain within their comfort zones, entrenched leaders hang on to old, non-working forms. Many still hope that what worked yesterday will work today. Church people sanctify and calcify ministry forms into articles of faith. Any move to change them becomes a holy "call to arms."

The price tag is high. Form should follow function, but in most organizations it does not. Whether it be neglect, laziness, ignorance, or enculturation, church organizations are becoming monuments of maintenance. This must not continue. The church needs to be liberated from this slavery to administrative forms and released to its biblical, ministerial functions.

Bureaucracy is eating the heart out of the American church. Anguished church leaders ask me whether we can save the evangelical church. Is it worth saving? They see traditional structures standing in the way of fulfilling mission. Administrative overload is causing discouragement as it makes the simple complex, the easy hard, and joy a drudgery. Necessary decisions take far too long. Proposals for change are dead-on-arrival, killed by committee analysis and micromanagement. Structure can be our best friend or our worst enemy. In many cases, it has become our mortal enemy.

In most cases, Christians intend for their churches to reach people. They long for a better way, for change that will facilitate mission. The fault often lies with the leaders who do not know how to lead their churches through change.

We can compare this situation to a football game. The church's mission is to advance the ball, or the Gospel. The contemporary church does not field its best team. The first string, with talent and dedication, is busy taking tickets, selling programs, walking the aisles, selling refreshments, and counting gate receipts. We have tied their hands with red tape and kept them off the playing field. In churches today, administration and support ministries preempt front-line ministry to people.

Our churches are not organized for growth and fulfilling their mission. The mission must come first, but in most contemporary churches, policy and rules come first, and these are organized for security, predictability, and safety. Congregational involvement is negated. How many safety nets or layers in the decision-making gauntlet do we need?

How can we make sure we do not make a mistake or that no one person will lead us, get too powerful, or take personal initiative without permission of the group? Church leaders are fed up with a tradition allowing the ungodly and immature to have as much clout as the elected leaders. Yet congregations demand that they have input on issues ranging from pastoral selection to mission dollars. History testifies that multiple administrative layers provide no insurance against stupidity. Stupid people find ways to be stupid regardless of the system. Satan makes certain fools find loopholes for their foolishness.

Lyle Schaller states it well. "The greater the emphasis on empowering lay volunteers to make the critical decisions in administration, the more likely that it will be a small congregation averaging fewer than two hundred at worship."[2] What is wrong with a church of two hundred? Nothing, in itself. The issue is that many of these churches could be larger if they were truly reaching people for Christ. The reason many languish, without reaping any harvest, is that they are locked up by a traditional administrative system. The mission with the biblical mandate is being sacrificed on the altar of tradition.

This bureaucratic pathology believes it is good to involve more and more people in administrative decision-making as the church grows. But the opposite is true! The larger an organization becomes, the more that administrative decisions should be delegated. The church should not broaden its administrative base, it should expand its ministry base. It must streamline its structures by removing administrative layers, reducing the number of committees, shrinking the time involved in administration, and limiting the number of decision-makers.

Congregational churches, as opposed to elder-rule churches, suffer more from heavy structure than other forms of polity. And nearly all churches are congregational. In his essay, "The Rise of the Evangelical Conception of Ministry in America," Sidney E. Mead argues that the tendency in all of America's churches, even the ritualistic and sacerdotal ones from the Old World, has been toward congregationalism.[3] People find ways to express their views and cast their ballots. They can vote with their tongues, their checkbooks, their attendance, and other creative means. All polity, including the elder-rule context, must deal with congregational input, response, and desire, though congregational churches make it easier for people to express their views than the elder-rule church. The only difference between them is the instrument for choice determined by the denomination. The outcome, however, is the same. The congregation gets its way, one way or the other.

Not only is administrative overload frustrating the leaders, but the multi-layered, pyramidal organizational chart that is the pattern in most churches communicates control and inefficiency. To those forty-five and younger, who are emerging as leaders, this lack of efficiency cannot be tolerated. These baby boomers have learned that the higher up you send a responsibility, the longer it takes to be done, the more political entanglement you have, and the more it costs. If churches are going to reach this particular group, there must be change.

We have a serious problem: the system no longer works. Before we explore the critical issue of administration, let's look more closely at the system as it has developed.

Rural Roots

Since most of America was rural two hundred years ago, the roots of our congregational system are rural. This system worked well for many years, and still does in some rural communities. But we are now an urban culture. The problem is that, just as missionaries tried to force American culture onto Africans and failed, well-meaning churchmen have tried to make urban-suburban churches conform to the rural church mode, and they have made a mess of things.

By its nature, a rural community was small with few people spread over a large land mass. This agrarian culture fostered an informal, family-oriented lifestyle. People knew each other and knew a great deal about other people's business. There were very few secrets. They knew a person's foibles, his strengths, his business practices, and his family life.

Back then, church practices made sense. One such practice was the selection of church leaders. A small congregation came together and chose a nominating committee from the floor. Since everyone knew just about everything there was to know about each other, it did not seem important to have qualifications for the people who would nominate the leaders. When the slate of nominees was presented, no one was surprised. Everyone already knew who the nominees were because the decisions had already been made in the parking lot and down at the Koffee Kup Kafé. The church was a close-knit community. It was family, with all its faults and magnificence. Familiarity was the safeguard against pollution of the system.

At first, when cities were extensions of towns, and churches were small, the system continued to work. But cities began to grow, and Americans started moving away. Television took over, and people stopped talking to one another. They moved off their front porches and surrounded themselves with hedges and walls. As the churches grew, the members carried the informal system of leadership with them. Members became uncomfortable as strangers joined the church. The system was flawed: People no longer knew each other, they were no longer family.

In this last decade of the twentieth century, we live in a cut-flower society without roots. When selecting church leaders, we are working at a disadvantage. We do not know one another very well. We do not know extended families, or business practices, or character, or integrity. The larger the church, the more formal leadership selection must become. This problem is compounded when church members must vote for people they do not know, who are selected by others they do not know. It breaks faith with the spirit of Scripture to select a committee casually without notice from the floor of a business meeting for selecting leaders (1 Tim. 3:1–19; Titus 1:5–8). A new paradigm is needed which permits us to change the structure while retaining its positive distinctives.

The rural system still works well in the small church. It calls for a minimum number of deacons, trustees, elders or board members. As a church grows, however, problems arise. Usually, the constitution calls for additions to each of the main boards. Normally, the various subsidiary boards convene and form a general or executive board. For example, suppose there are seven deacons, seven trustees, and seven mission board members with four to five main boards. When all the members meet together, they number twenty-five to forty people. This is cumbersome because the same decisions have been visited numerous times by the same people, in different forums. In addition, most decisions discussed by the deacon board are reviewed and voted on by the executive board and are then rehashed and voted on by the entire congregation! While a safe system, it is extremely inefficient. It wastes time and demoralizes those in leadership.

The high frustration level on the part of urbanites began when their churches grew and culture changed. A system that once worked for 150 to 250 turned into a monster when the church grew to 600. The membership expanded, and more committees were added, as the constitution required. The administration became massive, gobbling up willing workers into committees. It tied up its best people and kept them off the front lines of people-ministry. It fostered a clergy-centered ministry style with lay administrators as supporters. And it effectively cut the laity out of ministry. The larger this administrative workhorse grew, the more inflexible and formal it became.

The informal leadership selection process that has endured calls for selection of leadership by unqualified committees and more work with less information in an unknown environment, with the result that unqualified leaders are often chosen. The executive structure has grown until it has become like a king-size mattress with no handles: no one can grab it, and it keeps falling over. The unwieldy organization tends to smother the church, with leadership struggling and worn out, trying to get out from under it.

Another failed import of rural to urban was the traditional weekly schedule of a church. In rural, small-town America, Sunday was truly a day of rest. Farmers did not work, and businesses were closed more tightly than Jack Benny's wallet. It was a stationary society with no cars or television. So it made perfect sense to spend a good part of Sunday in church. There was time for Sunday school and worship, followed by a trip home for a family meal, conversation, and a nap. Then everyone was ready to return to church at the end of the day. Rural people worked long days, and the mid-week Bible study and prayer meeting was welcomed. Services on Sunday mornings and evenings and Wednesday nights fit the rural lifestyle.

Again, this system worked at first in the urban centers. However, attendance at the mid-week activities and the Sunday evening services gradually dropped. A number of reasons contributed to this decline. The most important was technology. The advent of television, home videos, and their accompanying toys, captured the public's imagination as well as its time. No longer could church activities measure up. Another reason for the drop in attendance was the mobility of society. Travel became part of people's lives. People wanted to get away from the stresses of life. Today, Sunday has become a day for Christians to "hit" church early and spend the rest of the day with family, in fun, excitement, and those extras that make life meaningful. The church is now competing with some very attractive options. Competition among the meetings within the church itself has also become a problem. The rural system essentially offered one kind of meeting in three forums. Sunday morning brought singing, praying, and preaching. Sunday evening was simply a less formal repeat. Wednesday evening was another sit-and-listen time followed by prayer. In urban churches, we have added adult Sunday school classes. Now, the parishioner has four meetings each week, which all meet basically the same needs. In the context of their jammed schedules, people select one or two items from the church menu. They no longer go to church three or four times a week. They no longer attend more than one meeting in the same week when it appears that these meetings are addressing the same needs.

This system creates unbalanced Christians, and it will not work. The mentality of the present system is management, not leadership. Its focus is maintenance, not mission. And it results in restriction, not release. Culture has changed, and so must our forms, if we plan to be relevant and effective and pleasing to God. The solution is to think function, not form. Churches must streamline and reduce administrative personnel. They must meet the changing needs of their members. If the church desires to move people toward mission instead of toward institutional maintenance, a new administrative model is needed.

12

Democratic Leadership Should Be Responsive Leadership

Egalitarianism is politically correct but practically wrong. There is a destructive notion afoot that all opinions are created equal. This is as silly as the flawed concept that all people are created with equal abilities. All people have certain rights before God and are equally loved and cherished by God, but some people are smarter than others, better educated than others, and endowed by their Creator with more talent and brainpower than others. Everyone should be given equal opportunities, but some will do better than others. Some are made to lead while others are made to follow. Any group, organized for any reason, will be composed mostly of followers, led by a gifted minority. This is true of the local church regardless of the chosen polity. Not everyone can lead, and if everyone tries, the results will be disastrous.

The thinking in a democratic, congregational church is that everyone has equal abilities and that all people at one time or another should be able to lead. This simply does not work. Too many churches have the wrong people in the wrong place because it was "their turn" to lead. A church family must define its roles. The nuclear family, whose members do not perform their roles properly, is dysfunctional. The same is true of the church family. An obedient church is one that appoints leaders who are gifted and spiritually suited for the task. Anything less is sin.

Let's look at the questions of a church staff member trying to clarify democratic leadership as defined by his senior pastor. "My second question goes back to your point that you follow a democratic approach to leadership. I'm still not sure what you mean by that. Do you mean the majority rules? Or do you mean participatory democracy? Or do you mean you lead with the consent of the members? Or do you mean that the initiative always rests with the laity, and the staff responds to their initative?"[4]

Leaders must lead, or they will be frustrated, ineffective, and emotionally deformed. A leader who is not permitted to lead is bound in a straight jacket, both functionally and emotionally. The many different kinds of leaders—charismatic, catalytic, managerial, transformational, authoritarian, and laissez faire—have one thing in common: They must lead or their purpose will perish.

A true leader does not live by the majority rules motif. He is first a servant of Christ and steward of the mysteries of God (1 Cor. 4:1). When the majority follows God's way, the leader goes too. When the majority does not, the true leader must disagree. A true servant/leader remembers he serves Christ first; he serves the people's best interest when he serves Christ first. Such a leader seldom waits for the congregation to take the initiative. He realizes that, instead of change, groups favor the status quo and the path of least resistance. This is why leadership is crucial. Leaders initiate, groups respond. Leaders make plans, groups follow plans. Leaders inspire, groups get inspired. Leaders cast vision, groups thrive on and work together toward the vision.

Leading and following are clearly different. Followers should seldom lead, and leaders should only follow as a form of training. The best leaders are those who were good followers in their younger years and have grown to view the principles of authority and submission as cooperative. While leaders remain in submission to authority, they spend most of their time leading. Democratic leadership is leading with the consent of the people. Once there is agreement that God has appointed the leader, the people must follow. A congregation must come to grips with the reality that it is not equipped to lead the church, and it must follow its leaders unless those leaders clearly violate scripturally based doctrinal or moral codes. This view does not permit "pickyunish" legalism, critical spirits, or a projection of congregational angst onto leadership. It does allow the leader to plan, strategize, initiate, and inspire. The congregation responds, gives permission, and supports. It also follows. Leaders and followers need each other. No organization can live long or well without both. Churches must celebrate the difference between leaders and followers and live by it.

Participatory Democracy

As Christendom's most revered church consultant, Lyle Schaller gives this view:

> The goal of a participatory democracy appears to be relatively easy to attain in the congregation of thirty or fifty or sixty members, especially if full participation is limited to adult males—but is that really a participatory democracy if women and children are barred from the decision-making process? This has been demonstrated for decades in thousands of small congregations, especially those that came from an Anabaptist tradition and emphasize the ministry of the laity. It is far more difficult to implement a participatory system of congregational self-government when the membership reaches one hundred and nearly impossible if the membership exceeds two hundred. The larger the size of the congregation, the higher the proportion of members who simply will refuse to invest their time and energy in attending ten or fifteen congregational meetings per year. *Likewise the greater the emphasis on participatory democracy, the greater the probability that the natural and inevitable distrust by the members will lead to a "split" as some of the members walk out to form a new congregation.*[5]

What many fear about stronger leadership is an autocratic dictatorship. Their concern is that giving any small group or elected board too much power can lead to serious error. This is a real danger—strong leaders can go wrong. The other side of the coin, however, is the danger of congregational paralysis. I believe that leadership by *Roberts Rules of Order* and political infighting have hurt the church far more than autocratic leaders. How many "church bosses" have orchestrated their will through the church constitution?

Autocratic dictators from the laity outnumber the clergy ten to one. The most likely critic of strong pastoral leadership is the "church boss" in danger of losing power. I see far more churches locked into disputes over "administrivia" than leaders who are out of control. If forced to make a choice, I would opt for strong leadership over a congregation trying to control its leaders. Leaders should be selected by their congregation and held accountable by the same, but they should be allowed to lead without hindrance within agreed-upon parameters.

I often hear people argue against strong leadership by citing some luminary who built a giant ministry empire and then went wrong. I certainly would not defend those who have sinned and shamed themselves and their Christ. I would, however, like to focus on the good aspects of their work. Which would you rather have: a person who (warts and all) was able to build a large ministry and introduce thousands to Christ, or the thousands of theologically correct, safe churches in our land who have failed to introduce a soul to Christ in years? Which is more dangerous to the cause of Christ? What is most grievous to the Holy Spirit? I will take strong leadership with its excesses and its spiritual harvest over controlled nonleadership without fruit. (Frankly, I am tired of listening to critics talk about excesses and abuse while they fail to see their own faults. Let's take the log out of our own eyes before we go after the splinters in the eyes of others.) I am not defending excess or abuse or sin of any kind. My question is, which is worse: reaching people for Christ in an imperfect way or not reaching people at all?

The church needs leadership. Congregations cannot provide it. They must rid themselves of the controlling mentality leading to an elaborate system of committees with a series of checks and balances. Churches have been too concerned with limiting authority, reducing power, and smothering initiative. The right plan is to release people, empower them to soar, and encourage their creativity. This is the positive focus.

Where does one draw the line between the authority of the congregation and the liberty of the leaders? Or to put it another way, how long are the leaders' leashes? The answer is, as long as the congregation allows. There should be a mechanism for the congregation to have input and, if necessary, vent its frustration with leadership. It needs to be written that the congregation can overrule its chosen leadership if necessary, but only as a last resort.

Even if the constitution does not call for meetings where votes are taken, the church should have forums of some type allowing meaningful input. Otherwise, group dynamics insist that the members will find a way, and this way very well may be contorted, perverted, and hostile.

Congregational Ownership

There are five issues on which every congregation needs input in order to have ownership in a church: (1) the calling of the pastors, (2) the annual budget, (3) selection of leaders, (4) facilities, and (5) membership.

THE CALLING OF THE PASTORS

The senior pastor's ministry touches everyone in the church. It therefore makes sense for a congregation to ratify its search committee's recommendation for senior pastor. It is not necessary, however, for associate staff to be called or voted on by the entire congregation. Secondary staff should be called in concert with the people with whom they will primarily work. The best example of this is a youth pastor, who can be hired by the board, based on a recommendation from the senior pastor with a hearty "amen" from students and parents.

THE ANNUAL BUDGET

If the congregation is expected to support the budget, it should have input on it. People will not support something on which they have never agreed and may not understand.

SELECTION OF LEADERS

The congregation should have meaningful and intelligent input into identity of its leaders. This is not done by nominations from the floor or choosing from a slate of officers put forward by a committee selected from the floor. The top leadership board should be confirmed by the congregation in an orderly and biblical fashion. (There is no need to elect all of the various boards; they can be appointed by the elected board.)

FACILITIES

Before new facilities are purchased or built, the congregation should agree to the commitment. It is foolish to think people will support major funding for something on which they have not been consulted. It is equally as foolish to ask a large group to be involved in the planning of such facilities. (Too many fights have erupted over such miscellaneous items as the color of the carpeting!)

MEMBERSHIP

If a church practices official membership, the congregation should ratify what a select membership committee has suggested. This applies to the dismissal of members as well. (It is vital that those bent on destroying the church be eliminated if unrepentant.)

The Enculturated Church

American Protestantism, as a democratic approach to congregational self-government, often tends to emphasize the rights of every member, including the right to have a voice and vote in every decision. This worldview has encroached on the church. Modern evangelicalism is entangled with democracy. It is not surprising, therefore, that the church is deeply enculturated. The tentacles of society have wrapped themselves around God's people. Christians generally do not understand the difference between congregational involvement and the democratic form of government.

The dangers to the church are manifold. Some of them can be explained by the work of Alexis de Tocqueville, a Frenchman who visited America in the 1800s. In his masterpiece, *Democracy in America,* he pointed out the differences between European and American views of democracy. Europeans, reacting against aristocratic society, saw the abolition of inequality in democracy. In western Europe, the choice was egalitarianism or totalitarianism. By contrast, Americans saw themselves as equal, and they tended to define democracy as the protection of individual rights.

When democratic theory and New Testament truth meet head-on, there is conflict. Let's look at four issues that arise.

EQUALITY

Not all opinions are equal. One person, one vote: This is a holy creed in the United States of America. All votes are equal. A farm worker's vote counts as much as that of a United States senator. This system is the best available in a pluralistic society with no agreed-on final truth. The church, however, does possess an agreed-on final authority, and it is not a constitution or *Roberts Rules of Order.* It is the Holy Scripture. Without this, we are hopelessly adrift. Scripture encourages us to listen to the wise and mature. Proverbs 3:1–6 warns us not to listen to fools or the immature (see also Prov. 15:5; 26:5; and Heb. 5:11–13).

The danger in a participatory democracy is that anybody can stand to his feet and influence others. People cannot see through bad advice. Both Scripture and personal experience teach this. The arrest and crucifixion of Jesus, the stoning of Stephen, the arrest and execution of the apostle Paul offer supporting examples. Christians are called sheep for good reason—they are easily deceived (2 Cor. 10: 3–5, 11:3). Many times the least spiritual is the most political. Many fools can work the system and hold up God's work to meet their own needs for power, attention, purpose, and something to do.

The church must protect itself from the foolish and anyone whom the enemy can employ to move the church off its mission and onto politics. Clearly, leadership needs to ferret out poor opinions from good ones. Some votes should be counted and others weighed. Some votes carry serious clout, and leaders should have input prior to voting. But the responsibility must fall on the shoulders of the leaders.

MAJORITY RULE

The majority is often wrong. Congregations can be influenced to do evil as easily as the mob outside Pilate's palace released Barabbas instead of Jesus. The French permitted Napoleon to lead; the Germans elected Hitler; and the Italians supported Mussolini. In biblical history, the majority wrongly rebelled against the authority of Moses, and ten out of twelve spies returned with the wrong report concerning the Promised Land. The point is that a congregation, or majority, can be wrong. White congregations have voted not to allow minority congregations to rent their buildings because the minority children "will scratch the ping pong table." Others have not allowed paraplegic pastors to serve because "it would not look good to have a cripple on staff." Some vote not to permit youth evangelistic concerts in the church because they might "dirty the sanctuary." The more a congregation is asked to lead, the more it will be wrong.

PERSONAL RIGHTS

Member obligation is a high priority; personal rights are not. When members begin to insist on their rights as congregational citizens, they are stepping out of Scripture into secular democracy. A person becomes a member of the church by means of grace, and every member should consider it a privilege. Self-denial and service should be esteemed (John 3:16; Luke 9:23–25). Members must support, follow, esteem, and pray for their leaders (Heb. 13:17). They should not criticize, politicize, lobby, or remove them (except in extreme cases). Then, the congregation knows its role, and the leaders know theirs. Roles, not rights, is the motif, coupled with prayer rather than politics and service over sedition.

CONGREGATIONAL CONTROL

Leaders are not called to represent the congregation. Tocqueville argued that excessive emphasis on protecting individual rights closes the door to truth, beauty, and good. This is seen today in our country where the emphasis on individual rights now erodes the value of excellence. Extremism to the right or left leads to the same destination. If we go to the extreme and protect everyone's individual rights, we deny basic human rights. If the right controls and censors, we end up with Orwell's big brother fascism. Conservatism in the extreme is fascism with a "goose step"; liberalism in the extreme is fascism with a smile.

Leadership's role is to liberate people to fulfill their potential. Any leadership that focuses on securing a certain faction's rights will dull the organization's cutting edge.

The representative form of leadership is highly political, reduces priorities to the lowest common denominator, and creates unnecessary friction at the leadership level. Too many congregations view their leaders as representatives of the various viewpoints that bring balance to church life. Truth becomes a negotiated commodity driven by politicized opinion, and the greatest good is institutional peace, translated "keep everyone happy." This is impossible to do, of course, except in the absence of biblical conviction. The Bible directs us to keep the motivated focused and at work, while institutional peace demands that the immature and unmotivated be at peace. This denies the needs of the motivated and caters to the least committed. We cannot do both and remain faithful. We must be driven by Christ-commanded activity, not a consensus-driven, synthetic truth.

Leaders must first represent Christ and his Word. They must first be stewards of the mysteries of God. They must know and obey the Scripture as servants of Christ. Then they can listen to what people say. This is vital to successful leadership, especially in biblically unclear matters.

It is possible that important truths can be revealed through the congregational will. Please, however, do not confuse congregational wisdom with God's revelation. Do not allow the fallible to change the infallible. Congregationalism does value and allow participation, but it is not democracy. Democracy is part of enculturation. I believe it is a pollutant in the church. While congregational input is good, democracy in a church is bad.

Participatory Decision-making

If you said mustard, I would say hot dog. If you said pastor, I would say parishioner. If you said board, I would say bath! There were many nights after a six-to-eight hour board meeting that I was saved by a hot bath. Thirty minutes in steaming hot bubbles, and I was fine. The very thought of trying to work difficult decisions through a group of people governed by *Roberts Rules of Order* gives me a headache. While I still have no love for administrative meetings, I have found a way to remain positive.

I am indebted to Kennon Callahan for his explanation of a workable, liveable, decision-making process. "There is a direct correlation between decisionmaking and structure. A solid participatory decisionmaking process contributes to a streamlined organizational structure and a streamlined organizational structure facilitates solid, participatory decisionmaking."[6]

In participatory decision-making there is a spirit of openness and trust. The input of members is welcomed, but they don't have to be involved in every decision. The number of people involved in a decision is determined by the number of people impacted by the decision. It is vital to anticipate the level of controversy. How strongly do people feel about the issue? Will it cost a lot of money? Will it require a wide participation level in dollars as well as energy? What is church tradition in these matters? How credible is the leadership? What standing does the pastor have? Most people do not want to be in on every decision. They do, however, want access to leadership and the opportunity to give input. When leaders act as though they have something to hide and do not value congregational opinion, watch out! Then the congregation will want to vote on the color of Sunday school chalk. In the environment of participatory decision-making people trust the leadership. Most decisions are made informally and are simply ratified in a formal meeting. This is the setting most conducive to getting things done.

The Decision-making Process

Solid decisions are characterized by agreement with the intentional mission of the church. When a decision does not meet this criterion, it must be seriously questioned. Why would a church decide to move in a direction different from its mission? There are many temptations to make knee-jerk choices, especially in crisis or under pressure to please the disgruntled.

The purpose of participation is not discussion. The process must facilitate decision-making, which is not usually accomplished through long, tedious discussions. Long discussions only signal poor preparation. When leaders have done their homework, prepared the congregation with preliminary, printed information, and provided forums for questions and answers, the formal discussions should be short and sweet. Committee chairmen around the world need to learn this lesson. Solid decisions characterized by wisdom meet needs. They are not prisoners to zeitgeist—the spirit of the age.

Those who love Christ and the church can express their differences in small forums provided by wise leaders. The process is effective when, in the midst of conflict, the opposition can respond to one another in mutual trust, respect, and integrity, bringing honor to Christ. Those who insist on performing in front of the entire group have another agenda. Many of these are seeking an audience and trying to whip people into an emotional lather in order to get their way. (May their numbers decrease, their tribe die, and may they attend another church!)

Ineffective Congregationalism

The purpose of the organizational structure is not to involve people. This is a harmful and destructive myth. In a dying church, committees provide the way to gain status. In a living church the members want to get through the administrative tasks so the job can get done. The purpose of the church is to involve people in God's mission. Administration is not the game. Effective churches conserve members' time by developing streamlined organizational structures.

Kennon Callahan gives the following advice: "Twenty percent of the decisions made in the local church are strategic and will accomplish 80 percent of the results."[7] This 20 percent should be the best and brightest decisions. The other 80 percent are tactical, not strategic. They can be delegated to task forces, groups, or committees. Give 30 percent to key leaders and chairpersons of committees. Another 50 percent should be given to smaller groups and specific individuals. Delegating decisions nurtures a feeling of ownership and openness. It makes the church more grass-roots in its practice, with those close to the action making the decisions. Those working within their sphere of ministry are endowed with the responsibility and the authority.

This contrasts with the traditional, congregational model, which insists on formalizing all decisions and holding an official vote by those who do not care or are not qualified. This is controlling and inefficient. It cuts out those involved in the actual doing of the work. This means that 20 percent, a usual quorum, vote on 100 percent of the votable issues. These are often those who show up out of habit for such meetings. Many of these people have no real understanding of the issues on which they are asked to vote. A better plan is to have the entire church vote only on that 20 percent concerning the entire church, as suggested above. The church can be congregational without poisoning the water with democracy. And there can be meaningful input as well as speedy decisions.

A good friend and former associate of mine shared his angst concerning congregationalism. "I am afraid that the two years I served as church chairman ruined it for me," he said. "I don't want anything to do with the organized church. I have lost my spiritual passion, and I wonder if the institution is anything like Christ planned." This man began leading with passion for Christ. He is now one of thousands who hang around the edges of the church out of duty or for the sake of his children. What causes such great repulsion? Is a bad church reason enough for dropping out? To answer these questions, let's look at three common complaints: the improper use of God's people, the waste of time and energy in decision-making, and the tolerance for deviant behavior.

Improper Use of God's People

The proper use of God's people is to train them for the work of ministry (Eph. 4: 12–16). Although the church has been very effective in keeping people busy, it has done a poor job of training for ministry. Leaders have corrupted their calling and abused those entrusted to their care. They have made the institutional church their master and have enslaved followers to religious busy work, at the expense of the mission and calling of the church.

The scene of the crime is usually policy boards and administrative committees. For example, a congregation of 400, using the rural form of congregational government, would have a number of standing boards: elders, deacons, trustees, missions, Christian education, general, and women's ministry. These would be supplemented by other committees such as worship, social concerns, evangelism, preschool, long-range planning, and others. If each of these were to meet monthly, if no one served on more than one board, and if each committee required seven members, then 202 people would be needed to administrate the church. Let's assume that this sample church averages 300 adults in its worship service. Then a full two-thirds of the active adult congregation would be required for administration. Since 202 adults are not about to involve themselves, 78 people must carry the load.

Add to this the other ministry involvements required: choirs, women's groups, Sunday school teachers, kids' clubs leaders, youth workers, Evangelism Explosion, sound booth workers, and ushers. Let's assume these programs require 184 workers. Now, the total administrative need is 438, but the church has only 300 on its active role! (In a letter to me, a pastor sent these actual figures.)

This church's pastor might express his frustration in these terms, "We need to simplify organizational structure by eliminating boards and ministries that are not serving the purposes of outreach and discipleship. But where do we begin? We are creating new positions without eliminating those older ministries that are no longer effective. There are many ministries, but few are being done with the type of excellence that attracts and holds newcomers. People are reluctant to serve on boards. They tell me, 'It's a waste of time. It's boring. It serves no real purpose.'"

Sadly, this situation is typical. The baffling truth is that, even though this style is a graveyard for ministry motivation, those abused by it will fight to the death to preserve it. Like abused children and spouses, they enable the abuser by not facing the destructive reality. Additionally, few can dig out of this "administrivia" and frustration to create new ministries. Churches like this one struggle to lift up their eyes and see the fields ripe for harvest.

This is institutionalism in its most destructive mode. When the work of administration keeps the church from its mission, the administration must be reduced. It is an evil that must be eliminated. If we are not willing to streamline bureaucracy to reach people, then the mechanics of ministry have become the ministry. This is idolatry.

Waste of Time and Energy

Another common complaint in today's churches is how much time and energy is wasted on decision-making. I remember often wondering why the church board discussed such questions as whether a new lawn mower should be purchased or how many Good News gloves should be placed in the lobby. Seemingly endless discussions droned on about the pulpit clock, placement of trophies, the offering plates, and the right kind of fertilizer for the lawn. None of these topics should appear on the leadership board's agenda. These are lower level decisions for trustees and janitorial staff.

Many congregational churches are actually autocratic and controlling while claiming to be open environments where people have the last word. In truth, the environment is restrictive and smothering. In these churches, the top board insists that every decision be made by it. Subsidiary boards function only to kick the product of their labor upstairs. Everything is controlled by those farthest from the action—the church board.

What is wrong with this? It wastes time. It takes too long. It gives too much power to the leadership. It devalues people's work. When a subcommittee's suggestion is rejected, its members become disheartened. Not only is this ineffective, it abuses those on the committees. Leaders should have authority based on their spiritual leadership, not on administrative power, which in the end is nearly meaningless.

Tolerating Deviant Behavior

If a seeker wants to see the current spirit of an evangelical church, let him attend a business meeting. Such an experience would send most away, convinced there is no substance to the Christian message. Young, vibrant Christians stay away from such meetings because they are shot through with arguments, trivia, and power struggles. Power hungry "dunderheads" who get their religious jollies by politicizing the church dominate the talk.

Many church members have lived, or are now living, in an environment where the unspiritual and disobedient stand in the way of what God wants to do. They know the pain of being blindsided by a cloak-and-dagger interest group. They know what it's like to have those who attend in name only return and vote against whatever the leadership recommends. They know the devastation of whispering campaigns and the slander and gossip permitted under the guise of congregationalism. They know the sleepless nights before and after congregational meetings. They have experienced the delusionary joy of thinking they were finally over the hump. These members feel uncomfortable in environments where unspiritual, hostile, and bitter people with axes to grind can start serious conflicts. They either want to reduce the opportunity for the thoughtless and troublemakers to have an influence, or they want out.

The need to reduce the opportunities for spouting off and to increase the channels for intelligent, studied input is tremendous. There is a way to do this while maintaining an open, responsive environment. Leaders must seek a balance. This means fewer open meetings at which anyone can talk about an issue never before considered. It means more precise, smaller forums to cover single issues.

Ministerial Congregationalism

Our first responsibility to God's people is to prepare them spiritually for ministry and equip them in ministry skills. Anything less is unacceptable. It wastes time and energy to make simple decisions complex and short matters long and to include twenty people in a decision requiring only five. Allowing too much unholy nonsense to exist in the decision-making structure is destructive. Little patience or mercy should be shown to the power hungry church politicians. Do not allow the disobedient to dictate church direction. Make sure the hostile and bitter are not allowed to hold up progress simply to justify their own sin.

Kennon Callahan defines the solid, participatory decision-making process: "Solid decisions are made, ownership and openness to all opinions are high, the process is as important as the decisions, and the organizational structure is streamlined and constructive."[8] This means the church is organized to facilitate ministry. It means fewer people in administration, more on the front lines, fewer meetings, and more ministry. Administration supports the overall mission. It plays a secondary role to mission.

One need only traffic in evangelical circles to understand how often administration is paramount. Too many churches have their strongest leaders overseeing the facilities and managing the money. When people think about leadership, they think about those in charge of facilities and money. This usually turns out to be leadership-by-checkbook. God's will is determined by monthly financial statements—success is making budget. If our strongest leaders remain here, the church will institutionalize at "warp speed." Responsible, trained people are needed in these areas, but these can be faithful nonleaders. The first team should be engaged in ministry of the Word and in prayer, outreach, teaching, and other people-related assignments. We must liberate people to minister to other people. We must move out of our comfort zones and experience God's call, rather than the Christian humanism now dominating evangelicalism. *I advocate a ministerial congregationalism supported by a streamlined administrative congregationalism.* What do I mean by this statement? Let's look closely at it.

Ministerial congregationalism: All disciples are ministers. Paul clearly teaches that every Christian is endowed with a spiritual gift and is set apart for ministry (Rom. 1:1–7; 1 Cor. 1:26; 12:3–26; Eph. 4:12–16). Believers discover complete fulfillment by finding their gifts and using them in the service of Christ (1 Peter 4:10–11). In the church setting, people are supported, encouraged, and trained for ministry. From there, they can interface with the world in a powerful way and penetrate their personal networks for Christ. *Ministerial* means that the purpose of all administration is to facilitate the mission for Christ, fitting together scriptural values and cultural realties as well as releasing maximum numbers to people-related ministry (2 Cor. 5:18–21).

This means that the members will be fully employed in people ministry, which is the top priority of service in the church. Administration gets a seat on the bus, but it is a back seat. This involvement contrasts with the more traditional paradigm. Traditional congregationalism values large numbers of people serving its administrative and policy-making agencies. I advocate a scripturally driven type of congregationalism in which leaders and followers find their greatest purpose (Eph. 4:12–16; 1 Cor. 12:12–16).

Supported by a streamlined administrative congregationalism: Administration must support, not dominate or dictate the mission. The church must organize for mission, not maintenance, by streamlining administrative duties. What is needed is less administration and more decisions made by those involved.

Following Callahan's observation that 20 percent of decisions yield 80 percent of the positive results, the top church board should act on the 20 percent, or the crucial issues. The other 80 percent should be delegated to the grass roots who are more directly involved with the issues. A general cannot make a foxhole decision for his infantryman. Such a decision must be made quickly, for it is a matter of life and death. The foot soldier better understands the context, has more of a vested interest, and can implement his decision immediately. The same is true in churches. We should centralize the crucial 20 percent that touches everyone and spread the 80 percent among the troops in the trenches. No official meetings need to be held, or votes taken, or forms filed. The foot soldiers simply act, and do, and see results. This makes the elected board's meetings shorter and more strategic. It empowers those closest to the action with the authority to make those decisions that make a difference. After all, they are the most qualified and will make the better call. This transforms administrative work into productive decision-making. Centralizing 20 percent of the decision-making means fewer people making decisions and more people implementing them so that people are more involved with people and less tied up in meetings. The larger the church, the more necessary this becomes. Otherwise, procedures and policies eat away time from the real ministry.

Authority

Congregationalism means that the congregation should have final authority at the local church level. This authority is crucial. Let's explore why. Regardless of tradition, it is vital for the authority structure of the church to be clearly identified. To argue that Christ is the final authority is not good enough. Every church needs Christ's power and presence, but these can only be experienced subjectively. They take effect objectively through delegated authority. The clearer the authority structure, the greater the facilitation of mission.

The purpose of authority is to influence human behavior and provide behavioral parameters. In the New Testament, the word *authority* means power. Scripture teaches a spiritual power available through the Holy Spirit, who empowers God's people to meaningful action. Leaders empowered by the Holy Spirit provide accountability in exhortation, encouragement, and correction. They give vision, strategy, and shape to the mission. If leaders lead correctly (1 Peter 5:1–6) and the congregation ministers properly (Heb. 13:17), the body will mature exponentially (Eph. 4:16–17).

Two clear biblical truths support the need for authority: Human nature demands accountability, and the divine nature is resident in all believers.

Because accountability is needed, final authority should rest with a group rather than with a single individual. With the passing of apostolic authority, the early church located its authority in a group of elders. It makes no difference whether elders oversee an entire city of churches or a local congregation. The principle remains the same: The authority rests in a group, not an individual. (An exception to this concept is the papal authority practiced by the Roman Catholic Church. Another is those mission organizations in which the final authority rests in a single founder or president.)

Accountability should keep leaders and followers from making serious errors. When people operate in an authority fog, there are accidents. Regenerate disciples still sin, and desperately sick hearts are capable of ugly actions (Jer. 17:9). Each believer can have the mind of Christ, but even a disciple's mind is corrupted by sin and limited by humanity (1 Cor. 2:9–16). This is the reason for accountability in a congregation.

Group authority comes from the priesthood of each believer (1 Peter 2:9; Rev. 1:6; 5:10). This doctrine posits the possibility that God desires to work directly with the believer, that a piece of the divine nature is resident in every disciple. The proposition is that people, in touch with God through prayer and the Word, can discern his will (Heb. 4:14–16). If we believe in the priesthood of all believers, we must also believe that Christ's presence can be manifested among them, that God can and does express his will through the ordinary follower. In fact, Christ promises to be present in a special sense when people gather in his name (Matt. 18:20).

The three loci of power in the church—the congregation, leaders, and staff—must provide checks and balances, which facilitate mission. I suggest this simple interface: Final authority rests in the congregation; delegated authority in the leaders; and daily authority in the staff.

Final authority in the congregation is based on the reality of human nature and the potential of the divine nature. The congregation provides protection and counsel to its leaders. It keeps them from leading the entire group into a theological or moral abyss. Congregations cannot lead, provide strategy, establish vision, or formulate long-range plans. They must delegate these activities. The congregation should understand its role and not infringe on the role of its leaders. It should not attempt to lead or manage. When not in session, the congregation commits to follow its chosen leaders. When officially gathered, it fills the role of final authority over its leaders.

This authority structure frees the leaders to assume their proper role of *delegated authority*. They are charged with filling their leadership duties and knowing their boundaries. They should develop strategy, provide vision, and appoint task forces and committees. They should model corporate values and teach people to obey by personal example (Matt. 28:20; Luke 6:40). They must be committed to Christ and sensitive to congregational desire. The tension here is normal. Leaders must acquire good input from their people and combine this input with scriptural commands.

The chosen leaders usually exercise authority on a monthly basis. The congregation's input comes officially only one, two, or four times a year. The church staff, however, must exercise its delegated authority *daily*. That authority is given by the congregation and board in specific understandings with each staff member. In particular, the senior pastor is given the responsibility to lead. As a gift from God to the church, he must give his full attention to this. He must provide vision and direction based on God's Word. His ideas and visions should be scripturally based and congregationally discerned. (Most congregations will gladly follow a leader who loves Christ and them.)

In short, the pastor reports to the board, the board to the congregation, and the congregation to Christ. What happens when a conflict arises? There must be an appeal process. The pastor should be able to appeal to the congregation to break any stalemates. The leaders should have the same right of appeal when they are unable to work with the pastor. But this process should be used only in emergencies as a last resort, when all else has failed.

Three-Level Administrative System

After the authority issue is settled, the church must move on to cutting the administrative fat. The goal is to *get as few as possible meeting as little time as possible for administration, so as many as possible can have as much time as possible for people ministry.* Doug Anderson puts it this way: "The more decisionmaking groups a church has, the more time they all have to spend defending who has the right to decide and how all those decisions will intermingle with each other and less time they have to spend in people ministry, our mission of disciplemaking."[9]

The multi-layered church administration no longer works and is a waste of time and God's people. The multi-layered, pyramid organization communicates control and inefficiency because it is controlling and inefficient. The higher you kick a decision, the longer it takes to get done, the more political entanglement you have to untangle, the more it costs, and the less effective the decision is when it finally occurs. Many multi-layered congregationalists think congregationalism gives power to the people, but nothing is further from the practiced reality. The more layers, the more powerful and controlling the top elected board becomes. People are less free to decide, act, implement, or have intelligent input. Such a hierarchy cultivates restrictive thinking and stifles vision. A structure encouraging vision is the great administrative need of the church.

There are very few tasks that require monthly meetings, and the power games and political baggage that go with them. The church needs to get rid of all standing committees between the top elected board and the grass roots. This means that trustees, deacons, and mission boards would cease to exist as standing committees. Their functions would continue but in a different form. Money can be counted and deposited and records kept by appointed individuals without monthly meetings. Facilities can be maintained without meetings. A five-minute phone call is sufficient to accomplish simple functions now requiring elections, board meetings, unnecessary discussions, and agonizing, tedious debates. Where does it say that meetings must be held to administer the material and financial matters of the church? Certainly some meetings should be held, but they need not be numerous and long.

Empower the people as task forces and have them meet as needed. For example, the board can appoint a key person to head missions, someone who is not a board member but a mature believer possessing the right qualifications. This person forms a task force with whomever he needs to work with him. The task force meets when necessary to carry out its mission, and when its duties are done, it ceases to exist. This works. It is a mind-stretcher for many, but it releases the congregation from administrative overload.

Three levels constitute this administrative system, instead of five or six. The first level is the elected board. The second is the task force leaders. The third level is the grass-roots workers. The key to such a system is the ability of the elected board to recruit, delegate, and hold appointed workers accountable. This structure eliminates most of the tedium and the unnecessary bureaucracy now dominating most churches five years old or older by getting as many people as possible involved in working and helping other people. The goal is to "de-bureaucracize" decision-making. Humanize it by on-site decisions about people (not things) and ministry decisions relating to the mission (not administrative matters concerning the material world). Then there will be immediate results that advance the kingdom of God. It can be done. Why not try it!

The "Off-Campus" Ministry

Shrinking the administrative base and expanding the ministry base requires another paradigm shift. This time it involves a change in the administrative model. Jim Peterson provides a helpful teaching tool on this shift in his excellent work, *Church Without Walls*.[10]

In this book, Peterson also develops the idea that at least half of ministry is "off campus." Building on this, I theorize that the purpose of "on-campus" ministry is to facilitate this "off-campus" ministry. A paradigm shift is required to move the almost exclusive "on-campus" thinking among evangelicals to an "off-campus" mentality.

Present-day evangelicalism is far too enamored with "on-campus" success. This thinking values the number of people who come to the temple for the ritual. It esteems conventional success rather than real results. The true measure of success is what the congregation is doing 95 percent of the time when they are "off campus." The church must stop associating success with what happens "on campus." It must stop focusing on buildings, crowds, pews, pulpits, money, and the "full-service church" delusion.

The world has stopped coming to church. There are no commands for the unbeliever to attend church. There are, however, many commands for the believer to go into the world and to live out his faith among the unbelieving population. A few evangelical luminaries have succeeded in getting disgruntled believers and seekers to attend church. But the vast majority of churches do not succeed, nor should they. The church should not sit and wait for the world to come to it. This is self-delusion.

Does this invalidate "on-campus" ministry? Of course not. We could not be the church without it. What, then, should be the purpose of this "on-campus" ministry?

Support "off-campus" ministry through administration. God has called and gifted some people to work "on campus," in administration and finance. These are godly servants who support the larger mission and enjoy the nuts and bolts of the work. Their work serves Christ and others.

Encourage and train others for "off-campus" ministry. Worship, counseling, training in ministry skills and Bible teaching are "on-campus" ministries crucial to the effectiveness of "off-campus" work. These are necessary to train and help people live well for God. "On-campus" ministry in perspective is not an end in itself. It must be lean and efficient, preparing people for the real action taking place "off campus."

For the new paradigm to work, *the mission must come first!* Paul states that we have been given the ministry of reconciliation (2 Cor. 5:18). Jesus prayed for us not to be taken out of the world, but to live in the world and stay faithful (John 17:15). We are to go to the world; it will not come to us.

Improving "Off-Campus" Ministry

The evangelical church has not fulfilled its mission. We have done a great job of removing ourselves from the world. The irony is that we have removed ourselves socially and physically from the world while allowing ourselves to be thoroughly discipled by the world. We are now reaping the poor harvest of what we have sown.

There are three ways to improve our "off-campus" ministry. The first is to *focus on real results.* This means living with integrity in word and deed among an unbelieving people. It also means penetrating social, institutional, and relational networks by proclaiming the gospel and giving people a chance to make decisions for Christ. It includes discipling new believers in the "off-campus" environment and helping them harvest their personal networks for Christ.

The church can design small group communities to assimilate new believers without insulating them from those they want to reach. The church is the church when it exists and lives for others. Churches with this mentality will not be insulated, pulpit-dependent, or disobedient. What a wonderful place to be!

The second way to improve "off-campus" ministry is *to staff and pay for it.* What if half the church staff and budget was directed toward this ministry? Recently, some members of a church asked me what I thought about the role of their second pastor in full-time "off-campus" ministry. I told them it was the best idea I had heard all year. To make such a transition requires time and study. When a church spends most of its money on itself and its staff and its programs, it violates the spirit and calling of Christ. Why be dysfunctional when Christians can be faithful disciples who have died to the world and given themselves to Christ and his mission?

The third means for facilitating the "off-campus" ministry is *training.* People do not automatically know what to do when exhorted to reach their world for Christ. It is crucial to teach them. Leaders must lead the way by showing others how it is done. If leaders are not modeling off-campus ministry, it becomes the Achilles' heel in that we talk about it but don't train people for it. The pastoral staff and board members must pick a mission field and go after it. They must take one or two others with them who will be able to reproduce the particular model. Some will know enough to do it on their own, but most will not. The model will include task forces empowered with immediate, grass-roots decision-making ability. These task forces report back through an agreed-on system to keep everyone accountable and energized. Once others are trained, the original leaders can manage the process as it reproduces. The principle is to model the process to apprentices who will then reproduce it and manage it.

Conclusion

For renewal to take place in the church today, we must be willing to sacrifice nonproductive forms for productive function. Bureaucracy is eating the heart out of the evangelical church. Simple decisions take too long. Our best decision-makers get swept up by an overwhelming administrative current. Too many churches are governed by their own idea of democracy, locked into a system that does not work.

I strongly advocate a ministerial congregationalism supported by a streamlined administrative congregationalism. Such a system employs all church members in people ministry and places administration where it belongs—as one part of the overall picture. It also enables the church to organize around its primary objective, mission. The idea is to get as many people involved in working with and helping others as we can. This is vital for renewal of Christ's church.

Part 6

We Must Create Community

or

Grow Big by Staying Small

All the believers were together and had everything in common.

Acts 2:44

13

The Small-Group Community

Can the contemporary evangelical community change its ways and move toward true, biblical *koinonia*, or fellowship? I believe it can if we commit to making disciples by creating communities.

Christians need community. "If we are to use the word community meaningfully we must restrict it to a group of individuals who have learned how to communicate honestly with each other, whose relationships go deeper than their masks of composure, and who have developed some significant commitment to rejoice together, mourn together, and to delight in each other."[1]

What many churches call fellowship, however, is nothing more than superficial "pap." Talking about the world and the weather around a coffeepot once a week does not qualify as *koinonia*.

There are different kinds of communities within the church. One is the **conceptual community**, of seventy-five or more people who gather around concepts, dogma, or creed. This community normally manifests itself as a church worship service. Another is the **fellowship com-**

munity of seventeen to seventy-four people who focus on fellowship. This is usually an adult fellowship or Sunday school class.

If I had to choose a community, I would choose the **small group**, numbering from three to sixteen and characterized by intimacy. Its members share life together on a deep level. This chapter focuses on this small-group community and its importance in the process of disciplemaking.

My thesis is simple: *The small group of five to sixteen members is the best forum for creating community; it is also the optimum environment for making disciples.* Since the mission of the church is to make disciples through evangelism (Matt. 28:19–20), then all churches serious about disciplemaking and world mission need small groups. Disciples cannot be made without accountability. The strongest and healthiest context for such accountability is the love and support that small groups provide. The small group must be carefully structured with definite goals if it is to fulfill its mission. An important role of the small group is to move people through a variety of spiritual statures to maturity. Often pastors and churches have no effective means of discipling people to spiritual maturity. In many churches the pastor tries to do all the training and nurturing. That leads to making small what God meant to be big. It limits the church.

The Moses Mentality

The trap that caught Moses is the same one that snares thousands of dedicated Christian leaders. Moses spent each day counseling endless inquirers. The congregation of two million kept the leader very busy. Jethro, Moses' father-in-law, observed the leader's wise counsel, his extreme dedication, and his servant's heart. But Jethro was disturbed by what he saw, and he challenged Moses.

"What is this you are doing for the people?" Jethro asked. "Why do you alone sit as judge, while all these people stand around you from morning till evening?" (Exod. 18:14). Moses replied defensively, "Because the people come to me to seek God's will" (Exod. 18:15). They need me! Moses was saying. I walk and talk with God. What do you expect me to do? Turn them away?

It is easy to do what comes naturally, especially when it builds our ego, elicits praise, and promotes a good cause. Moses' managerial blunder has become commonplace among contemporary, well-meaning leaders. His ego kept him from seeing the need to delegate responsibility. This oversight was disobedience. His method was not the best way to meet the people's needs. It did not build leaders, and it was self-destructive.

Does this sound familiar, pastors? The Moses Mentality says, I am responsible for all my people's needs, even if I must work eighty hours a week. The seductive power of this kind of thinking is evidenced by the fact we honor those who exhibit it. In so doing, we pay homage to disobedience and award leaders for missing the mark.

What was wrong with Moses' style? It was his own. Does God have a preferred method? Yes. The story of Moses illustrates what I mean.

Moses' Style

Moses did for others what they could do themselves. Because of his heavy work schedule, Moses was blinded to this. Being buried under a pile of work not only grinds a person down physically and emotionally, it robs him of time to gain perspective.

Moses worked alone and did not train anyone to replace him. Leaders who work hard without commitment to training and multiplication leave big holes of unfinished work. Once they are gone, there is no one to pick up the load. As modeled by Christ and taught by Paul in 2 Tim. 2:2, this simply is not God's will.

Moses wasted talent. The people stood around Moses from morning till night. Many leaders like having an entourage tending to their physical and emotional needs. But adoring courts have no place in Christian ministry. Many argue that most pastors or leaders do not have such groups. What about the congregation who praises its hardworking pastor, a one-man band, who can do it all, and does? This congregation sets the stage for its pastor to be the lead actor in its religious drama. When it comes to real ministry, these people are, in the words of Jethro, "standing around."

The work was too heavy, and Moses was sure to wear out. Jethro predicted that Moses and his followers would wear themselves out. The people would eventually tire of waiting for help and would end up with unmet needs, and Moses would be exhausted.

This is the choice facing the contemporary church. We must share our work load through training and multiplication or live with vast, unmet needs. In order to meet these needs, both inside and outside the church, we must change the pastoral paradigm into one where the workload is shared. This does not mean creating more committees or having lay people do the religious "grunt work." It means sharing the crème de la crème—those choice assignments. Hundreds of people can lift more ministry weight than one or a few. If we attempt the Moses Mentality, then we diminish God's church and his mission, which in turn quenches the Spirit.

Jethro offered Moses some advice on responsibility. The parallel to the New Testament is clear and encouraging (1 Tim. 3:1–16; Eph. 4:11–16).

God's Style

Select capable people. Jethro stated the qualifications necessary for selection: "Select capable men from all the people—men who fear God, trustworthy men who hate dishonest gain" (Exod. 18:21). The selection process should be based on an objective system that is fair to all. As mentioned in Part 3, careful study and prayer should be invested in any selection of leaders.

Teach the team members. Before those with right qualifications could be successful they had to understand the decrees and laws as Moses understood them. Moses had to show them how to live, and he had to teach them the skills and duties needed for problem-solving.

Again we see the importance of modeling. Successful reproduction and delegation require the selection of the right personnel. The next step is showing the personnel the way to do the tasks and then permitting them to practice the skills under supervision. Once this happens, they will truly be trained for the assigned work. Ignorance of such basic concepts has short-circuited thousands of promising missions. A church that cannot reproduce quality leaders and ministry cuts off its productive future.

Jethro suggested a way to divide the responsibility: "Appoint them as officials over thousands, hundreds, fifties, and tens" (Exod. 18:21). This breakdown represented the optimum structure for training new leaders. Each new leader would start with ten, then move to fifty, to one hundred, and finally to one thousand. Those who were faithful with little would be promoted (Luke 16:10; 1 Cor. 4:2). Ignoring these principles is like playing with a bad referee. You can play well yet still lose because of the ineptness or bias of the referee. I recall a frustrating experience I once had. My college basketball team played an arch rival in a hostile environment. The officials calling our game were local businessmen and friends of the opposing coach. In order to win, we not only needed to play better, we had to beat them badly enough to get these officials taken out of the game. We protested their outrageous calls. In frustration, we called them "homers," a pejorative term for unethical referees. They continually called technical fouls on us. The more we protested, the worse they got. Although we were easily the better team, we lost the game.

Poor leadership creates the same frustration. You can come up with superior ideas and innovative strategy, but if your leaders are not trained and tested, they will not have the background, character, and will to adopt the ideas and implement the strategy. The beginning of good leadership is proper selection and attention to the details of training. Pay the price to select and train well—it's a good investment.

Getting Started

If church leaders want effective platoons of determined believers working together to reach their networks for Christ, then small groups are the way. If leaders want a fair system that finds and equips other leaders, and if the pastor wants an army of ambassadors committed to the ministry of reconciliation, then small groups are the way. Small groups are the best forum for creating the community necessary for accountability and disciplemaking.

Establish a Beachhead

How does the pastor or church leader get started? Let me suggest several priorities. The first is to establish a beachhead, or group of potential leaders, aimed at creating a disciplemaking environment. That beachhead must start a pilot small group. The key to beachhead theology is knowing the right beach, or choosing the right potential leaders.

Regardless of the selection method, those chosen must have willing hearts with teachable spirits and a desire to identify with the church's philosophy of ministry. In one situation, I spent six months asking for the names of people who would make good, small-group leaders. In other cases, I started open discussion groups that anyone in the church could attend. In these groups it became clear who were potential leaders. If the church was family-oriented, I selected three or four couples as possible leaders. In every case, I was headed toward the same destination: the formation of a prototype group in which I could show the members what I wanted them to do with others.

Orientation

The next step is to invite the potential leaders to your home for dinner and orientation. When I did this, I explained why I had invited them and why I thought they were the best choices. Not only did I look for teachable spirits, I also searched for those who had the respect of the congregation and the time, interest, and gifts. (It helps if some are official board members, but this is not an absolute necessity.) I asked these potential leaders to pray about investing six months of working with me in a prototype experience lasting a predetermined period of time. The long-range goal would be to launch several groups duplicating the experience of our group. There would be weekly leaders' meetings at first, followed by meetings twice a month.

THE PROTOTYPE

The purpose of the prototype is for apprentices to experience the group and learn the skills essential to group success. I would model everything from directing a Bible discussion to leading prayer, from drawing out needs to building community. The team members would learn by doing these things and by taking turns leading the group. They would also team together in evangelistic outreaches. We would hold each other accountable for the various projects and help each other over the more difficult assignments. This shared experience raised the chance of group success. There is no substitute for learning through participation.

The Leader's Credo

A small-group leader's credo is *do with them what you want them to do with others.* The same credo works equally well regardless of the system or tradition. (I have employed it in three very different churches. The first was a somewhat traditional, five-year-old church, which had 125 in attendance; the second was very traditional, fifteen years old, and numbered over 500; and the third was a rather avant garde church-planting project, which eventually reached over 500.) The greatest sin of small-group start-up is violating this credo. Leaders do not seem to have the patience or commitment to begin correctly. If we accept the thesis that small groups create a superior environment for making disciples, then we must invest the time and effort and commit to starting right. To begin with more than one prototype is a big and costly mistake. The credo is based on the premise that it has already been determined which prototype will best serve as the heart and soul of your small-group family. This is the kind that must come first, because this lays the foundation for everything else.

Customize the Group

A third priority for getting started is **customizing the group**. One restaurant invites customers to "build a breakfast" and "customize" their meals. This can be done in the small-group setting as well. Rather than locking into a set of materials or programs, build a group and customize it to your particular needs. I recommend developing a set of principles to guide you. If the group is to be short in duration and light in commitment, develop one set of principles; if long in duration and heavy in commitment, another set of principles is used. You may have six sets of principles providing the basis for six kinds of groups, with some relating to every group.

Build a group that supports your primary objective of keeping people growing to be like Christ. The preamble to building the group must be knowing the objective. Any group's primary objective must include mission. Most groups implode because their mission is too small. A group that only reaches into itself will become self-indulgent and insular. Examples of other, secondary objectives include training people to witness, studying the Bible, understanding biblical teaching on finance, supporting those in crisis, and reaching out to a need group.

Disciplemaking is another clear objective. Your heart-and-soul group must score a direct hit on meeting its objectives.

Should the group be open or closed? Both the "meta church" and cell-based church models maintain that all small groups should be open: Anyone can come. Open groups intentionally try to reach new members. A closed group, on the other hand, is one that accepts no new people for the duration of the group, once the mission is stated and the members are secure.

Several years ago, the Fuller Institute of Church Growth conducted a study on this issue of open versus closed. A large number of pastors were broken into two groups, A and B. All pastors in Group A agreed to consolidate their adult Sunday school classes for the same age group. All pastors in Group B agreed to separate their Sunday school classes for the same age group into three classes. After a certain length of time, attendance was taken. Almost without exception, the number in each consolidated group declined while the number in each separated group multiplied.

Dr. Richard Myers of the Church Federation of Greater Indianapolis had years earlier verified this principle and recorded it. It appeared in the American Baptist filmstrip, "Let's Face It." Myers Law can be stated like this: "The church grows both in number and in meaningfulness to its members as the number of face-to-face groups increases."[2] In other words, a church does not grow by getting more people into the same class or small group; it grows by adding more classes or small groups.

There are two important corollaries. The first is that "a church grows numerically as the number of outreach or open groups are multiplied."[3] An open group that is proactive, or intentional, will reach outsiders. And the second corollary is that "a church will grow spiritually as the number of inreach or closed groups are multiplied."[4]

Open groups such as those modeled by the huge churches in Korea, Singapore, and South Africa provide unlimited possibilities for growth. Those who advocate the open group as the heart and soul of small group community do so because open groups are better than closed groups for accomplishing outreach and numerical growth. I do not argue with this. I believe a good share of small groups in a church should be open. However, I see them playing a supporting role to the basic group. Let me explain.

The closed group works best as the first group for the following reasons. An open group cannot provide the necessary structure and accountability. It will lead to large numbers of untrained and undisciplined people. In a closed group, the members commit to such specifics as time frame, skill development, and outreach. Everyone shares the learning experience at the same time and at the same level.

A second reason for the closed-group structure is to provide an atmosphere for mastering and living with the spiritual disciplines. A strong group structure is crucial in the early stages of developing the spiritual disciplines, which are required for effective Christian living. The reason so many Christians bear so little fruit is this lack of discipline. The average Christian dabbles in the disciplines, then gives them up. In today's environment of sloth, consumerism, and light commitment, more structure is needed. Repeated actions made possible by external structure form internalized habits, and this leads to true freedom. As Vance Havner said, "The alternative to discipline is disaster."

Third, you can deploy group graduates to lead open groups from the closed-group environment. You now have people steeped in the disciplines who can teach those who are less committed. Open groups, populated by Christians at various places in their spiritual pilgrimage, need a highly skilled leader to monitor and lead them. Spiritual and numerical growth will result.

When open groups are the only kind of small group in the church, and people at various levels can be in the same group, mediocrity will result. It's like throwing everyone in the shallow end of the swimming pool; everyone thinks that staying in the shallow end is normal. A few people will venture into the deep end. Maybe some will learn the backstroke or the breaststroke; some might even start diving off the edge of the pool or from a diving board. A few may engage in exciting exploits, but most will stay in the shallow end because it is easy, comfortable, and not strenuous.

People need groups that step them up in commitment. Each group should have a special focus and should challenge its members to do things that are uncomfortable and that will lead them to the spiritual maturity they desire. This cannot be accomplished with only one type of open group. This also leads to a self-directed spirituality. Spirituality is then defined as "meeting my own needs." This reminds me of the spirit of the age in the Book of Judges, where everyone did what was right in their own eyes. Self-directed spiritual development is a lousy idea and avoids the spiritual disciplines that should be common expectations for every Christian.

One of the great challenges of having every group an open group and essentially the same is that it requires leaders to be multifaceted in their managerial style. They need to be able to manage a seeker, a person with a broken marriage, an individual with theological questions, another person who wants to study the Book of Romans, and yet another who has a heart for evangelism and outreach. Even a well-trained pastor would have difficulty attending to the differing interests, levels, and directions of the group, and it would be nearly impossible for the lay minister. There will always be exceptions, but generally, this is an uphill climb that is too steep for most people to scale.

Basic Principles

There are five basic principles for any small group, along with a variety of options within each principle.

Be intentional. In addition to a clear objective, you must avoid the trap of promising more than you can deliver. Rather than telling people they will become biblical examples of mature disciples by joining the group, promise them that, if they keep their commitment and give themselves to the process, they will be on their way to a lifetime walk with Christ in two years.

Provide structure. Your statement of purpose and covenant provides a solid structure. The covenant gives the objective and speaks about such specific assignments as attendance, participation, and even coming on time. It also explains the leader's responsibility to help the members keep their commitment to God and the group.

Most people joining a group do not have spiritual discipline, such as regular Bible study, prayer, community living, accountability, and personal witness. Since character is the accumulation of habits, developing good habits takes place through repeated action. A group structure helps people develop good habits and reach their goals.

Strive for intimacy. The group needs to move from the structural foundation to one of love and support in which the deepest form of accountability exists. Intimacy allows people to know personal truths about one another. It allows them to confess their sins (James 5:16), request prayer, and create an environment of admonishment (Rom. 15:14) as well as encouragement. As Paul said, "Warn those who are idle, encourage the timid, help the weak, be patient with everyone" (1 Thess. 5:14). True freedom is found only within a context of love and support. If I think you love me and want me to succeed, I will listen to you. I will consider it safe to tell you who I really am. I know that I will not be punished for revealing such information. The group must reach intimacy in six to nine months or it will break apart. Tragically, many do not make it.

Insist on outreach. Every group needs a mission outside itself. Outreach projects protect the group from self-absorption and implosion. Without outreach, Bible study becomes academic, prayer boring, and fellowship turns superficial. Outreach provides a catalyst for spiritual development and should be included in the group's covenant. It energizes the group, injecting a vitality, which keeps the group inviting and dynamic. The late Karl Menninger said the best cure for depression is to roll up your sleeves, cross the railroad tracks, and help somebody.

Jesus taught that reaching out to others is essential to meeting one's own needs. In order to find purpose for oneself, one must deny self. This biblical truth is fundamental to discipleship (Luke 9:23–25). We must say "no" to self in order to say "yes" to God. Groups, therefore, must reach out corporately. Biblical foundations for evangelism along with training in evangelistic skills need to be included in the group experience.

Commit to reproduce. One of the advantages of small groups is their potential for rapid growth. Through a carefully managed apprenticeship system, groups can expand quickly and with integrity. Healthy Christians reproduce, healthy churches reproduce, and healthy small groups reproduce. When properly managed, the principle of reproduction can permeate the entire small-group network. Groups will not reproduce, however, when the expectation is absent. Poor training of leaders, a lack of long-range strategy, and lax management will cause the group to lose its missional integrity. But reproduction produces leaders.

In order to facilitate reproduction, each group should designate its start and finish time. Sometimes, in order to be faithful to our mission, we must do what does not come naturally. Moving away from a group with which one is happy requires the supernatural. Time frames that fit the group's mission benefit everyone. Some groups can fulfill their mission in six weeks, some in six months, and others in two years.

Healthy small groups combine every element necessary for growing healthy, reproducing disciples. They offer spiritual nurture and support, ministry skill development, accountability, training in outreach, long-term relationships, and worship. They develop leadership skills and provide the best people-gathering instrument the church possesses. Small groups within a church provide the emotional nerve center of the congregation. Most members call their small group "home." The small group is the best forum for creating community and the optimum environment for making disciples.

14

The Theology of Small Groups

The biblical basis for the small group is the Christian need for community. Let us look at four examples.

The Perfect Community

Before time and space, the Triune God lived in perfect community. God the Father, God the Son, and God the Holy Spirit have existed from eternity in perfect unity and communion. Their teamwork in creation is well documented. "Then God said, 'Let us make man in our image, in our likeness'" (Gen. 1:26). When Jesus left the heavenly environment, this perfect community was altered. When he became sin, it was smashed (2 Cor. 5:21). This is why Jesus agonized in Gethsemane and later cried out, "My God, My God, why have you forsaken me?" (Matt. 27:46). Community and relationship form the core of the universe and creation. They were modeled by the Trinity.

The First Human Community

Although Adam lived in a perfect environment, one essential need was not met. God determined, "It is not good for the man to be alone"

(Gen. 2:18). Once Eve had been formed, Adam existed in the most intimate form of community. Humans need to relate to one another in a close relationship. Otherwise they feel detached, displaced, and devoid of identity and meaning.

Community is still needed even when it is imperfect. Living in community involves sacrifice, emotional investment, and pain. But living without it is worse. Christian community is the attempt of Spirit-filled believers to restore some of that perfect community known only to the Triune God and the first family before the fall.

The Community of Jesus

When Jesus called his disciples to be apostles, he did so "that they might be with him, and that he might send them out to preach" (Mark 3:14). Jesus clearly correlated relationship with task. He called the men into community in order to see them confident enough to take the Gospel forward. The essence of community is belonging. His twelve disciples lived together in a small community and experienced redemptive relationships, those into which people have paid the price of emotional and material investment. Jesus modeled acceptance for them by allowing them to remain with him in spite of their periodic, sinful ways.

This kind of acceptance is, of course, the support and accountability the contemporary church should provide. Jesus knew that community does not come in the form of large groups. A group needs to be small enough for everyone to feel comfortable and safe, yet large enough for a variety of viewpoints. Jesus lived with his followers and left them with these instructions, "A new command I give you: Love one another. As I have loved you, so you must love one another. By this all men will know that you are my disciples, if you love one another" (John 13:34–35). Unless Jesus had called these men to community and modeled it for them, they would not have been equipped to obey his new command.

The Early Church

The first church started with 120 praying, expectant believers stuffed into a small room for ten days. With a rush of wind and a dose of the supernatural, they became 3,000. No longer did they fit into a normal room. Yet, we are told they were unified, their needs were met, and they were experiencing community (Acts 2:42–47). The modus operandi of the first church was to meet together in the temple court and in homes. By necessity, the apostles divided the people into organized groups, using a team of elders to communicate and execute plans (Acts 6:1–7). It would be safe to assume that the community they enjoyed came in the form of small groups. The apostles passed on what they had been taught. Small-group communities were the only possible way the apostles could track the needs and handle the issues.

The contemporary church can look to this example as the best method for knowing and meeting needs. Because of this environment, Luke could write, "All the believers were one in heart and mind. No one claimed that any of his possessions was his own, but they shared everything they had. . . . There were no needy persons among them" (Acts 4:32, 34).

It is difficult to find a renewal movement in church history without a small-group component. By the fourth century, Christianity had become both legal and corrupt. Wave after wave of monks attempted to bring life back to the faith by creating communities of commitment, sacrifice, and mission. They were reacting to the depersonalization of the institution. Basil the Great, Augustine, and Gregory the Great were entrepreneurial churchmen of their day. During the Middle Ages, the movement intensified, presenting protests, demonstrations, and alternative lifestyles to the church. The monks became the first "parachurch" expression. These men were courageous and creative, living on the edge and defining the issues. They arrived at this truth: You cannot effect change without organizing people into small groups and giving leaders the means to help them.

Martin Luther is well known for his courageous stand for the biblical doctrine of justification by faith. Few realize, however, that Luther understood that doctrine alone was not enough to equip the saints. In his preface to the Lutheran Mass, he suggested a little church within the larger church. Luther realized that effective Christian living is an unfulfilled dream unless you get people out of the pews and into communities.

Philipp Jakob Spener was a German who authored the *Pious Desires* in 1637. Troubled that the reformation was incomplete, Spener realized that right belief had not led to right living. He advocated small groups and suggested six activities for a small group: Bible study and prayer; renewing the priesthood of the believer; the application of faith, not just intellectual assent; breaking down of the clergy/laity gap; faithfulness of the clergy to the Word; and ministry of the Word to penetrate the unreached.[5]

Baptized by Spener, Count Nicholas Zinzendorf was a leader in building small-group community. Historian Richard Lovelace writes, "The most deliberate and successful use of the small group principle in history was the small band system of Count Zinzendorf."[6] Zinzendorf focused almost exclusively on the small-group community. Like the Puritans and the Pietists, he wanted to transcend theological and denominational differences and form a union of Protestants on the basis of a common recognition of godliness in one another. Lovelace says, "In many respects Herrnhut must be considered the most thoroughgoing and fruitful application of the principle of community in Church History . . . his success in turning Herrnhut into unified community through the linked use of prayer and small groups serves to demonstrate that Luther's original plan was viable. It also suggests a paradigm for the transformation of the whole church."[7] Lovelace concluded, and I agree, that "vitality cannot be present in the church until its macrocommunities and microcommunities consist of fully developed networks of Christians who are exercising their gifts and contributing to one another so that 'from him the whole body, joined and held together by every supporting ligament, grows and builds itself up in love, as each part does its work.'"[8]

Wesley's renewal instrument of choice was the small group. He created communities called societies, which met weekly in order to experience the spiritual disciplines of worship, prayer, confession of sin, Bible study, and accountability with respect to living for Christ. The members had to arrive on time. They began with singing and prayer. They were to speak with one another freely and plainly regarding the true state of their souls. The larger communities were called societies while the smaller groups of five to seven were named bands.

Jesus modeled the small group, and the first church instituted it. From monks to reformers to contemporary missions, each renewal movement has attempted community. Yet the organized, institutional church has militated against community and often smashed it. The true purpose of the church is making disciples, and this requires accountability. The church must provide an environment for positive accountability, and this is found within the small-group structure. We cannot allow the institutional church to destroy the true church.

15

The Tenets

T enet comes from the Latin word, *tenere,* meaning "to hold." Some of the following tenets have solid biblical support. Some are simply my opinion of what works well, a reflection of my experiences with small groups. These represent what I believe to be vital tenets to an effective small-group ministry within the local church.

Pastoral Leadership

As moral leader of the church, the pastor should lead the charge. This is what a congregation desires and expects. For a church to experience community, the pastor has to lead it there. The congregation knows how the pastor spends his time, and this shows them what he values. Small groups will never be a high priority unless the pastor has at least one hand on the wheel. Remember the small-group credo: Do with them what you want them to do with others.

Finding Time

Pastors face several obstacles in fulfilling this crucial role. The first is no time. Some pastors argue they do not have enough time and cannot add any more responsibilities. If this is your situation, sit down with your leaders and make a decision to delegate. Ask yourself what tasks are directly related to preparing people for works of service. You may be surprised to discover that some are not. Consider your scheduled preaching tasks (Sunday morning and evening, weeknight services), which require a large chunk of weekly work but meet only one need. It makes sense to drop one of those and replace it with a task to help people learn inductive Bible study. Work with a few leaders, teach them, and then let them teach others.

When C. S. Lewis wrote "only lazy people work hard," he was referring to leaders who abdicate the essential work of making decisions, directing others, establishing values, and setting goals. The hardest work to unload is that which we hold a "holy rationale" for doing.

Once you have learned the benefits of reproduction and delegation, you will have the time to expand into other needed areas. Train couples to do premarital counseling as well as hospital and home visitations. Train people in evangelization, follow-up of new believers, teaching the membership class, and doing other ministry tasks. If you can get work done through others, you will have experienced the fruit of the Ephesians 4 model, and you will have time to lead the charge.

We have time to do what we think is important. If you are serious about building community for the purpose of making disciples, you should invest time in small groups. Ask yourself what you want in five years. Do you want the same thing, only larger, or do you want a trained army of committed believers serving Christ effectively in the harvest field? If you're smart, you will see that the small group investment pays the best dividends of all.

Where to Start

A second obstacle preventing pastors from leading the charge is not knowing where to start. You start with both hands on the wheel. After you have laid the foundation for the small groups, become a manager. Obey the credo and do with them what you want them to do with others. This phase takes one year. You must choose a few leaders and take them through the prototype. By the second year, the groups are launched, and you can assume the role of leader in the leadership community. You can even delegate this particular task by training a lay person or staff member to manage the group.

Dependency on Preaching

The third obstacle is the pulpit. A pulpit-dependent church is not what God desires. It grows in direct relation to the preaching ability of its pastor, and this is not good. Such a church will die from its preaching. It has no reason to reach out. Dependency on preaching glorifies the pulpit and discounts other pastoral functions, making it impossible for the pastor to focus on the various aspects of teaching.

Today's pastoral paradigm is a leader who is focused on three issues: pulpit ministry; working and building leadership; and hands-on work with a small-group network. If you are a pulpit man, practice what you preach. Step out from behind the pulpit and commit to learning. People learn when guided into application through accountability and structure. Focus on training as well as the pulpit.

Basic Spiritual Disciplines

Your basic group must focus on basic spiritual disciplines. One scholar wrote:

> The New Testament church builds two other disciplines upon prayer and Bible study: the Lord's supper and small cell groups. John Wesley emphasized five works of piety by adding fasting. The medieval mystics wrote about nine disciplines clustered around three experiences: purgation of sin, enlightenment of the spirit, and union with God. Later the Keswick Convention approach to practical holiness revolved around five different religious exercises. Today Richard Foster's book, *Celebration of Discipline*, lists twelve disciplines—all of them relevant to the contemporary Christian. But whatever varying religious exercises we may practice, without the two basic ones of Emmaus—prayer and Bible reading—the others are empty and powerless.[9]

Don Whitney defines the basic spiritual disciplines as "personal and corporate disciplines that promote spiritual growth. They are habits of devotion and experiential Christianity that have been practiced by the people of God since biblical times."[10] Whitney lists such disciplines as biblical intake, prayer, worship, evangelism, service, stewardship, fasting, silence, solitude, journaling, and learning. Although a Christian can grow into Christlikeness without practicing every one of these, there is an essential core group. I consider this core to be biblical intake, prayer, worship, evangelism, stewardship, serving, and fasting. The functional purpose of the church is to glorify God by making disciples. This requires accountability. People will normally not have the perseverance to practice the above disciplines. Therefore, a structure is needed to support the accountability environment. And the best environment for such development is the love, support, and proximity of a small group.

Improved Pastoral Care

The small group community improves pastoral care. How? One way is through intimacy. It provides the best environment for expressing love and support. Given enough time people will feel safe and move beyond talking about news, weather, and sports. Men in particular need more time (six to nine months) to open up and share their real struggles. Research shows us that the most important counseling needs are love, empathy, and support. Ninety percent of what people need can be found in the small-group community.

This structure covers both crisis needs and general needs. Such a community provides people with ministry of the Word, prayer, and training. It also helps with material needs, friendship, and social life. Most people's spiritual and emotional needs can be met at the small-group level without the paid staff ever knowing about them. This method offers the one-hundred-member church thirty-five to forty caring ministers rather than just one. (Additionally, I have found that many of the laity are often more gifted, sensitive, and willing to meet the needs than the clergy!)

The traditional, pastoral care model has a 1 to 160 ratio. The average church in my denomination has 160 in its Sunday morning worship service. Even if a third of the group is children, the pastor has to work with over 100 adults. I suppose the pastor could remember every name and need if he devoted most of his time to that. It might also be possible for one person to keep up with 100 adults if he limited his involvement to crises. But what about the proactive issues of encour-

agement, training, and preventive counseling? What would happen to
them?

My argument with the traditional pastoral care model is that it puts
the burden on a few, denying the body the opportunity to minister as
well as a higher level of care.
The traditional model is symbolized by special clergy parking spots
at the local hospital. Only pastors can get into intensive care and see
patients any time of the day, regardless of visiting hours. I am not advocating eliminating the above hospital practices. I am, however, calling
upon churches to include more people in the process. Members need
to accept the ministry of the congregation as equal to that of the clergy.
Many clergy find much of their time spent traveling from hospital to
nursing home to afternoon teas. This is no more the primary responsibility of the pastor than long hours of counseling. A pastor's responsibility is to equip people to join him in such work.

I recall telling a congregation that my primary calling as their pastor was not to visit the hospital. Jaws dropped, arms crossed, and
faces twisted. My theology of pastoral care is simple. God has called
the entire body to care for one another (1 Cor. 12: 13–28; Gal. 6:1–4;
1 Thess. 5:14). Scripture does not give paid clergy specific hands-on,
caring responsibility. In fact, elders are charged with caring for the
flock (Acts 20:31; 1 Peter 5:1–3). Coupled with Ephesians 4:12–16,
these scriptures promote an organizational model followed by training. The clergy must be involved in these, but they must also train
others to do the same.

Developing Leaders

Small groups develop leaders more quickly. What is the best way to
build leaders? The answer is small groups. When your basic group is
focused on the spiritual disciplines, leaders will naturally surface.

Accountability and other demands of a spiritually disciplined group
sort out people. They eliminate those who are dabblers or unfaithful
or not ready for a serious commitment to Jesus Christ. One of my best
group leaders had to dismiss several people who would not keep their
commitment. These members appeared to be mature Christians, but
they were not.

It is quite common for churches to encourage the untrained, non-qualified, and unfaithful to lead. This is why the level of ministry in many churches is often so poor. Too many have allowed those with the power of the personality or pocketbook to elbow their way to the front of the church. A church without a system to test everyone for faithfulness is a breeding ground for "church bosses."

The small group community is not only the best place to raise leaders, it is also the best place to train apprentices. The group leader identifies an apprentice during the first six months of the group. That person then joins the leader in the leadership community, that special nurturing and training environment for present and future leaders. This apprentice is afforded the opportunity of working with the leader and then going out on his own. Character refinement and learning the necessary skills take place in the same loving, supportive community. Each apprentice can then lead his own group while the existing leader goes on leading others. The number of groups is multiplied with integrity. Every new group is led by a person who has been properly trained and tested before he is entrusted with the care of others. This provides the church with unlimited growth and the potential to reach those who have not yet been reached.

Support Groups

A support group is a special kind of group that is organized for people needing particular support. The goal of such a group must be that its members graduate from the group. A support group can itself become an addiction, perpetuating weakness instead of strength, and dependence rather than independence. In addition, the group leader must have had victory over his own problem in order for the group to work. While this does not mean perfection, it does mean the leader is on the good side of the addiction or behavior.

Support groups must not become the heart and soul of church ministry. One therapeutic church movement today is attempting to build ministry based on this kind of group. This is good, but support groups do not come close to building healthy believers in the spiritual disciplines. Even addicted, struggling Christians must eventually develop the disciplines, or they will be doomed to a life of slavery to their negative habits and beliefs. In addition, support groups cannot serve as a staple because they do not train Christians or produce skilled leaders and faithful servants.

A warning should be issued at this point. Be careful not to be swept away by the pervasive tide of the recovery movement. To those who are the true believers in the recovery movement, there are only two states that a Christian can be in: denial or recovery. Although there are some good things to be learned from the recovery movement, some of the things to reject are the ideas that everyone needs a group, everyone needs therapy, everyone has been abused or at least damaged by their parents and their background and needs to work it through. This is essentially humanistic nonsense that must be rejected by those who hold to a biblical worldview.

Conclusion

Because the most powerful accountability environment is love and support, an organized system for developing effective community is required of church leadership. The load of ministry is too heavy for one leader or group of leaders to carry. God's way of sharing this load is through multiplication. And this multiplication process comes through training and accountability. If a church desires growth both spiritually and numerically, then small-group community is the answer.

Small groups offer structure, intimacy, and outreach. They provide a training ground for the growing disciple by offering a place to focus on, and be nurtured in, the spiritual disciplines. The small-group environment also improves pastoral care by developing the priesthood of every believer. Small groups are definitely the best forum for creating community and making disciples.

Part 7

We Must Really Do Evangelism

or

Get Off Campus!

16

How Are We Doing?

Doing evangelism is different from preaching about it, talking about it, or even praying about it. While these are vital, they do not substitute for telling others about Christ. A year does not pass without the release of new materials on evangelism. Conferences, books, schools, institutes, and training methods are available to the church. Denominations and mission organizations have dedicated decades to global strategies for world evangelization. Seminaries have endowed chairs of evangelism. Yet, few penetrating words are being proclaimed by the church to the unchurched.

Some alarming facts have arisen. When asked to evaluate the impact of church growth over the last twenty years, church growth leader Peter Wagner said, "The percentage of American adults attending church has remained almost the same while Protestant church membership has actually declined."[1] A study done by Bob Gilliam found the average evangelism ratio of the evangelical church shockingly low. Under the sponsorship of Denver Seminary, Bob developed the Church Development Survey in which he surveyed more than 500 churches in 40 denominations over a 10-year period. This survey included more than 130,000 church members. The average evangelical church led 1.7 people to Christ for each 100 people in attendance. This translates into a church of 200 leading only 3.4 people to Christ each year. While some churches are doing well, according to Gilliam's study, most are not.[2] What has caused this evangelistic anemia? *Christianity Today* sponsored a survey designed to find out who was really doing evangelism. Those surveyed were not typical evangelicals. They were college educated, with an average age of 48. Half had been raised in Christian homes and 70 percent had been Christians for more than twenty years. The majority were Christian leaders; 31 percent were pastors.

James F. Engel analyzed the results. The definitions of evangelism fell into three broad categories. Thirty-four percent of paid church staff and 20 percent of the laity defined evangelism as communicating the plan of salvation and calling for a decision. One-third of the clergy and one-fifth of the laity restricted their definition to verbalization with a call for decision. Nearly two-thirds of the respondents defined it as communicating or sharing about Christ, his claims and his relevance. Twenty percent of those surveyed fell into a third category, defining evangelism as friendship or relationship building. Among the group, 93 percent said Jesus is the only way to God, and 89 percent believed evangelism is the responsibility of every Christian.[3]

One reason evangelism is weak is that people are doing what they think amounts to evangelism, but it is not true evangelism. Here lies the beginning of a theological erosion. While building relationships with the unreached is important, there is no biblical justification for calling it evangelism. The problem with "friendship evangelism" is that it is mostly friendship and very little evangelism. True evangelism always includes an intent to lead the person to Christ.

Another reason for weak outreach is that some people do not believe every Christian needs to witness. Eleven percent of the leaders surveyed question evangelistic responsibility. My personal experience confirms that well over 25 percent of the baby boomer evangelicals do not believe they are expected to verbalize their faith and call others to a decision for Christ.

Given the Great Commission, no thinking person would consider evangelism optional. The Bible-believing wing of the church has always taught world evangelism as a high priority. Most orthodox denominations emphasize it. Is every Christian responsible to verbalize his faith on a regular basis?

Five instances of the Great Commission are found in Scripture: Matthew 28:18–20, Mark 16:15, Luke 24:47, John 20:21, and Acts 1:8. This command was given to all generations. If we are going to lock onto the rights of the believer priest (1 Peter 2:9), we must also accept the responsibilities. Each must declare the wonderful news about Christ and sing his praises among the people. "That you may declare the praises of him who called you out of darkness into his wonderful light" (1 Peter 2:9). According to Acts 1:8, anyone filled with the Holy Spirit is going to witness for Christ.

Some people do better at evangelism than others. Some find it easier to give, or serve, or help, or pray. Biblical images picture the believer's posture as ambassador, alien, soldier, herald, and prophet. It is our responsibility and privilege to represent Jesus Christ in this present world. We are temporary visitors from heaven on assignment to communicate the Good News (2 Cor. 5:18–21; 1 Peter 2:11; Phil. 3:20).

Charles Spurgeon once said, "Though I can understand the possibility of an earnest sower never reaping, I cannot understand the possibility of an earnest sower being content not to reap."[4] The foundation of evangelism rests on Christians talking about what God has done in their lives. I travel a great deal and have many opportunities to share my faith. Sometimes I take the opportunity; sometimes I do not. The difference between these times is not a matter of emotion. If I waited until I felt great about God, the world, and myself, I would rarely witness. The real issue is whether I will take the opportunity to speak with this person or not.

Blocks to Evangelism

The *Christianity Today* survey also provides insight on the reasons people do not evangelize. It identified several major blocks to evangelism. Forty-nine percent of the respondents mentioned fear as the first reason for not sharing their faith. Timidity followed in second place with 45 percent. Twenty-five percent feared not being able to answer a hard question.

Fear

It is human nature to desire acceptance by others. It is our desire to be accepted and valued by God, family, friends, and work associates. Telling others about Christ is risky because it places our acceptance on the altar. Every time we speak clearly for Christ in an anti-Christian culture, our social and economic standing are at risk. Difficulties arise because we take rejection personally instead of remembering that it's the gospel people reject.

Overcoming fear is one part of learning to evangelize. "For God did not give us a spirit of timidity, but a spirit of power, of love and of self-discipline" (2 Tim. 1:7). Fear comes from the flesh or the devil. We overcome it by knowing God loves us. "There is no fear in love. But perfect love drives out fear, because fear has to do with punishment" (1 John 4:18). Our love for God and his love for us overcomes rejection and the natural fear of others.

The filling of the Holy Spirit conquers fear, too. Peter and John stood courageously before the Sanhedrin, yet fifty days earlier, they had been afraid. They faced their fears (Acts 4). Paul faced his fears also and asked the church to pray for wisdom and power in his witness (Col. 4:2–6).

Education on what works in evangelism can lower the fear level. Most evangelism comes through spiritual discussions with friends. General visits or talks finish second, and invitations to church third. Other common methods include prayer, friendships, literature, and invitations. In the *Christianity Today* study, only 1 percent said they used the salvation plan. Others did not because it seemed impersonal and threatening. (This is ironic since this is the means for an unbeliever to understand the gospel.)

Fallen Heroes

A huge 44.6 percent considered the moral failures of heroes of the electronic church as a major hindrance to witness. These respondents were affected by the ridicule aimed at the authenticity of the Christian faith. Skepticism about spiritual leaders in general, and clergy in particular, influenced them as well.

I personally have found all the "wagging" about such fallen heroes a facilitator to conversations about God. When people discover I am in the "God business," they like to address this issue. This opens the door for an explanation of the difference between the gospel, the Lord, and the excesses of some of his followers.

Time

Thirty-nine percent claimed they did not have the time to share their faith. It's hard to dispute this major hurdle to reaching others. Soft data is abundant. People are living in a time famine; time is in short supply. The facts do not support this, however. Hard data indicates that Americans have more free time today than ever before. Free time is the time left after work, commuting, care for the family, housework, shopping, eating, and other personal care activities. It includes the time spent participating in organizations, watching television, reading, visiting friends, and taking classes. Americans can now boast not only a forty-hour work week, but a forty-hour play week as well.[5]

Lack of Confidence

George Barna writes, "One dominant reason underlying the increasing reluctance of Christians to share their faith with non-Christians pertains to the faith-sharing experience itself. In asking Christians about their witnessing activities, we have found that nine out of ten individuals who attempt to explain their beliefs and theology to other people come away from those experiences feeling as if they have failed."[6]

Spiritual Discipline

Personal evangelism should be expected of every Christian, but it will not simply happen. It is a discipline and necessitates intentional prayer. Spiritual discipline is that consistent behavior taught by Scripture and essential to spiritual health and maturity. It is a commanded activity that should be built into our character. It calls for seeking God. It requires scheduling and making the most of every opportunity (Col. 4:4–5). It views witnessing as a loving act toward others. Jesus said, "If you love me you will obey what I command" (John 14:15). He commanded us to make disciples and be his witnesses. We must love God back by obeying him and sharing our faith.

The many different spiritual disciplines are developed within a structured environment that facilitates godly habits. Every Christian needs a structured boot-camp training in the basic spiritual disciplines, developing spiritual habits for promoting a lifelong godliness (1 Tim. 4:7). Christians have common needs, but if they are permitted to seek their own way, they will have little chance of fully experiencing God's plan for their lives. Self-directed spiritual development is a bad idea.

By dedication to the basic spiritual disciplines, a believer will have the ability to overcome the negative emotions of fear and doubt that hinder his witness. He will have the steadfastness of Peter and John, and he will be able to speak the Word with boldness (Acts 4:31).

17

Structure

The most productive way to involve people in evangelism is people-to-people ministry. We desperately need to liberate our best and brightest from administration and launch them into the mission field.

The findings of a recent survey confirm this. This study evaluated evangelistic effectiveness. Nearly half of the more than 1,100 churches surveyed returned a form. The results were calculated by experts at Baylor University. The study had an error factor of + or − 3 percent. The study found that the age of a church is crucial to evangelistic effectiveness.

Churches older than twenty years have an annual rate of conversions that is one-third that of churches under two years of age and 10 percent less than churches ten to twenty years of age. There are at least two reasons for this. A church initially reaches out to gather enough people to support a pastor and have church. Once this is achieved, its energy reverses from outward to inward. Church personnel are gobbled up by traditional church programs. The focus becomes institutional. The older the church gets, the more it becomes dedicated to survival for the sake of itself. This trend is creating the kind of deplorable evangelistic dearth that now characterizes more than half of our evangelical churches.

The second reason is pastoral expectation. Pastors must meet the needs of the saints, feed them, be their shepherd, attend their meetings, and live up to their expectations. The focus here is not on others, it is on self. The pastor becomes a chaplain. His focus is not outreach, it is servicing the saints. Church members do not want him to launch into the deep sea of local and world missions.

The survey found the rate of retention of new people is 20 percent less in these older churches than in those of two to five years of age. This is caused by those congregations maintaining they are open when in reality they are closed, and outsiders are not welcome.

The study also showed that pastors led 48 percent of the people evangelized by the church. Another interesting finding was that in larger churches pastors did more evangelism than in smaller churches. And, in the twenty-year-old churches, the pastor's evangelism ratio was 15 percent less than that in younger churches.

Pastors are not working through others to teach and model evangelism. They are witnessing but not reproducing. The pastoral paradigm is still dominated by the insular chaplaincy. Pastors remain in the office, often leading people to Christ in counseling sessions, confirmation classes, and church meetings. They are finding it easier to witness by themselves than build workable programs. And the older the church, the harder it is to change.

Many churches are now adapting their worship hours to the Seeker Sensitive Model. James Speer expounds on this model: "This interestingly represents a return to church-centered evangelism. At minimum it risks placing believers on a low-cal diet. At worst, it risks a distortion altogether of the meaning of worship—transforming it from an act of ultimate importance to an instrumental means for reaching the unbeliever."[7] When worship is reduced from an essential element in the believer's experience and is assigned to the duty of an outreach tool, danger arises. It takes what God meant to be paramount and places it on the secular thinker's menu as an optional item.

Changing Structure

Let me offer three practical suggestions for changing structure.

"Off Campus"

The first is a paradigm shift from "on campus" to "off campus." As we discussed in Part 5, the present church paradigm measures success by what happens "on campus." The problem is that those we need to reach are "off campus." Christians spend more than 95 percent of their time "off campus." This calls for a number of changes. Pastors need to minister more "off campus" and preach the new paradigm to the congregation. Leaders need to follow and provide training in creative "off-campus" outreach. The church budget needs to reflect this priority with a goal of devoting 50 percent of the budget to "off-campus" work.

The natural, biblical ministry flow is for Christians to go to church and prepare for going into the world. Christians should go to campus so they can minister "off campus." The powerful trend in the contemporary church is to reverse this flow. The problem, of course, has been that those who cannot make "on-campus" evangelism work are still trying because it is considered the paradigm of success. This paradigm is built on the old biblical structure of a scattered church bringing seekers into the church for evangelism. Most evangelism should take place "off campus."

Church-centered Evangelism

My second suggestion is a paradigm shift from individual evangelism to church-supported and church-centered evangelism. Beginning with pastors and leaders, the church must build a church-centered evangelistic mind-set. Christians need help in knowing how to be effective in their "off-campus" evangelism.

Dr. Paul Cedar, president of the Evangelical Free Church of America, has used and taught a workable evangelistic strategy for a number of years while minister of evangelism at Hollywood Presbyterian Church and as senior pastor at Lake Avenue Congregational Church in Pasadena.

This simple model covers all the bases. Spontaneous evangelism builds the foundation for personal outreach. The integrity of a person's spirituality is not overlooked, nor is the importance of prayer. The column labeled "Inviting" is something anyone can do. "Sharing" requires some training. Strategic evangelism focuses on equipping and

A Model for Evangelism through the Local Church

© Paul A. Cedar

	Spontaneous Evangelism (Witnessing)			Strategic Evangelism (Evangelism)	
Authentic Christian LIVING	PRAYING	INVITING	SHARING	EQUIPPING	DEPLOYING
1. The LORDSHIP of Jesus Christ •Luke 6:46	1. For WORKERS •Mt. 9:35–38	1. ANDREW •Jn. 1:40–42	1. RESPONDING to others •1 Pet. 3:15	Various Modules	
				VISITATION EVANGELISM	1) STRUCTURE 2) SUPPORT
2. The OVERFLOW of the Holy Spirit •Eph. 5:15–18	2. For YOURSELF •Col. 4:2–3	2. PHILIP •Jn. 1:43–49	2. ARTICULATING the Gospel •Col. 4:3–4 •Mk. 8:34 •Jn. 3:16 •Rom. 10:9–10	SPECIAL EVENTS	3) CONTINUING EDUCATION
				AFFINITY EVANGELISM	4) ACCOUNTA- BILITY 5) PRAYER
3. The FRUIT of the Holy Spirit •Gal. 5:22–23	3. For the LOST •Jn. 14:13–14	3. US!		OUTREACH BIBLE STUDIES	➤
4. The WITNESS of the Holy Spirit ◗ In WORD ◗ In DEED •Acts 1:8				TARGET GROUPS • Children • Youth • Senior Citizens	➤
				OTHER	➤

deploying. All church evangelistic events are important in establishing outreach priorities.

The change from "on campus" to "off campus" means evangelistic structures must facilitate the paradigm shift. The church would sponsor more evangelistic "off-campus" activities, both in dollars and time. This would require shutting down some boards and committees. It would also mean training leaders who model evangelism and willingly take the heat. This kind of thinking is new and threatening and strips conventional church leadership of its evangelical trappings.

Church Planting

My final suggestion is a paradigm shift toward church planting. One truth rarely challenged is that church planting is the best method known to reach the unchurched. It has a number of positive effects. One is that it expands the leadership base of the planting church. Many have bemoaned the fact some of their better, more seasoned leaders went with the new church, but this is good because other leaders must then step in and fill the void. It leads to twice as many leaders. Expansion of outreach is another positive effect. Once the new church is planted, the mother church is able to reach more people than it could otherwise reach. A new church is enthusiastic and needs people. Not only does it have an evangelistic motive, it wants to survive. New churches focus on people's needs and have fewer housekeeping chores, and, as a result, more people come into the kingdom. The fact the church plant is several miles away opens up new neighborhoods as well as new networks that would have remained untapped without the plant. A cleansing effect is the third result. Church planting requires a church to change people and structures. It accomplishes the much-needed elimination of bureaucracy and helps the church remain unselfish. Moving people around for the right reasons keeps the creative juices flowing and avoids stagnation.

This new structural paradigm has pastors seeing people scattered throughout the city doing ministry. They are thinking in terms of ministry results rather than activities on the church grounds. They look at more than their congregation's presence on Sunday morning. They see 100 percent of the congregation doing hundreds of ministry tasks. They measure results in terms of what kind of people their church is producing and what kind of teams it is placing on the field.

George Hunter III said it well:

> The western church needs to experience a paradigm shift that allows it to perceive that the traditional mission-sending nations of the Western world are "mission fields" once again. . . . To be specific, Western Christianity needs a multitude of intentional missionary congregations—churches that will abandon the Christendom model of ministry as merely nurturing the faithful—whose primary mission will be to reach and disciple people who do not yet believe. Many of our churches can be blasted out of their "edifice complex" by confronting ways in which we have entered a new apostolic age, akin to the situation faced by the early church's first three centuries of existence.[8]

I could not agree more.

18

Culture

Culture is comprised of those major strands of society that form the environment in which people live. It includes political and economic theories, religious beliefs, educational philosophies, and the arts. Social issues and foreign policy also come into play.

Today, the tentacles of society have a stranglehold on evangelical churches. Evangelicalism has been assimilated by the culture and is presently dominated by it. This sub-cultural environment has created a laissez-faire attitude toward the spiritual disciplines. It has also produced a legalism with respect to church forms, an acceptance of secular thought, and a doctrine of heaven and hell permitting optional evangelism. The political theory of democracy is so dominant that congregational churches are hard-pressed to identify the difference between democracy and congregationalism. Many of our accepted views are no longer scripturally based—they are culturally driven.

George Hunter identifies six watershed events that laid the philosophical groundwork for our present cultural milieu.[9] The first was the Renaissance, that period that rediscovered ancient Greek philosophy and science. This mode of thinking interjected "pluralism" into Western thought. Pluralism teaches that no final truth can be known.

It also believes that, if all world religions and philosophies were joined together, a synthetic truth would emerge. Hunter claims Christendom continued to come apart with the Reformation. Prior to this, the Roman Catholic Church dominated society. When the church divided, it lost its grip on Western thought. The church turned away from social management toward personal renewal and theology. The Renaissance and the Reformation combined to start secularization.

When the nationalistic spirit swept across Europe as a political force, Christendom's power ended. This Nationalism led to warfare among the nations. Empirical science challenged Christendom's assumptions about life itself. Three thinkers in particular hammered the Christian world view. Darwin negated creation, Marx questioned the need for religion, Freud redefined man's internal make-up and motives.

Built on the foundation of the Renaissance and accelerated secularization, "enlightenment thinkers believed that human beings are intrinsically good and reasonable, but that their environment makes them less good and reasonable."[10] This is why people believe human problems can be solved through education, jobs, a higher standard of living, and an egalitarian society. This is also why people think talking and reasoning together will lead to the elimination of nuclear weapons and even war. Enlightenment thinkers believe society can regenerate itself.

Hunter writes, "If the Enlightenment escalated the secularization process, urbanization, beginning in eighteenth-century Great Britain, stampeded it."[11] Urbanization speeds the progress of ideas because people live closer together. The more people interact, the faster they become secularized.

Secularization means removing God from public life. Richard Neuhaus's masterpiece, *The Naked Public Square*, powerfully supports the idea that God has been removed as a serious force in public life. If you remove God's name from the Pledge of Allegiance, Neuhaus writes, if you remove prayer from public schools and manger scenes from public property, and if you dismiss God as a major player, you will end up with a public square devoid of spiritual influence.

Christians who intentionally reach out to the unchurched know society is hostile to their message. One good example of such hostility is seen on television talk shows. An evangelical will be doing well, the host will be congenial, and the studio audience tolerant. Then someone asks the big question: What about the Jews? Are they going to hell if they don't accept Christ? Everyone freezes. If the evangelist has the integrity to say yes, the host and audience turn on him. Suddenly, he becomes a fundamentalist, a bigot, a Neanderthal, and "hayseed." How can anyone believe such antiquated ideas! This is what got us into slavery, Nazi Germany, and the KKK!

Phil Donahue, Oprah Winfrey, Geraldo, and other philosophical "junk food" vendors sell their wares daily to the American public. We live in a world where a movie entitled "White Men Can't Jump" is cute. But if a movie called "Black Men Can't Swim" were made, it would be considered racist. It is okay to verbally abuse a white, middle-class male (especially if he is an evangelical Christian), but to question the morality of a homosexual is considered homophobic. It is courageous to block a university's administration hall and protest support of the military, but it is dangerous and possibly fascist to place your body in front of an abortion clinic and protest the slaughter of the unborn. It is fine to say you're a civil rights activist in the league of the Civil Rights Movement led by Martin Luther King if you are gay, a feminist, an environmentalist, or saving a whale. Some abortion rescuers of the 90s are not treated the same as civil rights protesters of the 60s. Why? Because the secularized pop culture and the liberal media say anti-abortion thinking is outdated, religiously based, and politically incorrect. Good and evil are out; secularized pluralism is in.

Current Judeo-Christian thinking maintains that man is neither good or evil. Though not entirely Christian, this ethic teaches right and wrong, good and evil, and a transcendent origin. Moral codes are infinite and absolute. The abandonment of this Judeo-Christian ethic has led to the moral morass in which we now live. People are confused. In *The Closing of the American Mind*, Allan Bloom points out this moral confusion. The most crucial closing in society is the shutting out of the possibility of final transcendent truth. Today young people generally agree that no one can really know final truth. It doesn't exist.

One excellent example of this confusion was the recent riots and burning of South Central Los Angeles. A new moral ethic surfaced. Looters did not consider themselves criminals. Their deeds were not evil. They were simply expressing years of pent-up frustration and anger about discrimination. In reality what they were doing is what everyone under Satan's domain does—evil.

George Hunter offers a metaphorical, athletic image of Christians engaged in conflict with an enemy on the enemy's turf. I like this. Our labor for Christ is similar to a game on the road. Most coaches consider their season a good one if they win 50 percent of their away games. Road games are hard. The crowd is against you, the surroundings are different, the opponent knows the terrain and often plays better. Away teams do not expect favorable calls. I played and directed the Athletes in Action basketball team for five years. All our games were on the road. Because our mission was spiritual, we faced a challenge. At halftime, testimonials were given, and the gospel was presented. This often increased the hostility against us.

As Christians in this world, we are the "away team." Our secular culture militates against the Christian message and purpose. Satan is the god of this world, but he only has temporary domain (2 Cor. 4:4). We Christians are citizens of heaven, pilgrims; we are aliens on a special mission, ambassadors for Christ (2 Cor. 5:18–21). We should expect hostility and opposition. We must expect biased decisions by elected officials and the courts. It is tough to represent Christ in a humanistic culture. But, as Jesus said, "I have told you these things, so that in me you may have peace. In this world you will have trouble. But take heart! I have overcome the world" (John 16:33).

19

The Rumblings

The theological foundation for evangelism has slipped dangerously. This movement has not been an obvious one, such as from orthodox to liberal. It has been very subtle. The once solid foundation is now shaken by myriad questions. Is every Christian responsible for communicating the gospel? What is successful evangelism? Is hell a real place? Will good people go there? Does God torment unbelievers forever or does he simply "snuff out" their existence?

A harmful tradition within evangelicalism is currently weakening the foundation even more. It says a pastor/teacher should "prepare God's people for works of service" (Eph. 4:12). The principle here is good; however, a problem surfaces when it is applied. Many people do not know they have a gift for evangelizing others, and they will never know unless someone trains them. In most cases, that someone is the pastor. If a pastor is not willing to engage in evangelism and training, I question his call.

Should a pastor lead the charge? Will his congregation follow? *Christianity Today* asked this question of its readers. Their survey found that 54.4 percent of the pastors thought pastors were indeed the key. However, only 34.3 percent of the laymen thought pastors were the key.

Both pastors and lay people agreed that pastors played a key role in evangelistic interest and passion within the local church.[12] A study recently completed by Bob Gilliam points out a strong correlation between a pastor's behavior and local church evangelism. For this study, a statistic called a coefficient of correlation was used. This coefficient was either positive, between 0 and 1, with 0 indicating no correlation and 1 indicating a perfect correlation; or negative, with ranges from 0 to –1.[13]

Church Size	Correlation
largest	+.67
large	+.56
small	–.04
smallest	–.03

The data shows that, in terms of encouraging and empowering participation by members, the larger the church, the more important the pastor's own evangelism emphasis. When analyzing this data, Dr. Sharon Johnson of Baylor University wrote, "The correlation here is pervasive and strong. But in small churches the picture is quite different—the relationship is slightly negative. That is, in churches of 100 or less, greater personal evangelism of the pastor has a slightly depressing effect on the personal evangelism of the average church members."[14]

Several hypotheses support this finding. Strong one-on-one evangelism ability by a small-church pastor may indicate a lessened ability for training others to evangelize. The more time a pastor spends evangelizing may indicate he has less time to train. Smaller churches are often located in areas where the pool of receptive people is limited. If a pastor fishes too actively, church members may believe there are few fish left to catch, or they may feel the pastor is doing enough for everyone. It is very important for large-church pastors to model evangelism. It is also important for small-church pastors to train others in evangelism.

What tools can a pastor use to fulfill his responsibility? One is the "bully pulpit." "Bully" means influential, not meanness in spirit or imposition of will. An effective pulpit can create an environment that facilitates and thrives on evangelism and reproduction. It can set the priorities and the expectations. Evangelism can be preached from the pulpit, and people will know what God expects from them. "Bully pulpit" does not necessarily mean pulpit invitations. An invitation can actually be a negative experience. Some churches give weekly invitations with no results. This leaves the impression that nothing is happening in the church, and it can produce guilt. If people are going to be reminded of their need to evangelize, let it be through the positive motivation of a visionary exposition of Scripture.

The Gilliam study emphasizes the need for large-church pastors to focus on doing evangelism and small-church pastors to focus on training others to do evangelism. One should not be done at the exclusion of the other. By necessity, a large-church pastor either trains others or finds someone who will. A small-church pastor tends to do the evangelism himself because there are so few people to go around. In both cases, the pastor must lead the charge by modeling what is preached from the pulpit. If he wants people to reach their own neighborhoods, he had better be reaching his. If he wants members to bring the unchurched to worship, he should, too. If he expects people to rearrange their schedules, then he should set the example.

Dr. Allen Tunberg did a study of evangelical leaders. A good number of respondents consider agnosticism concerning the future state of the unevangelized a possibility.[15] The way this filters down is that God will work it all out. He is love, and he will not torment people forever, especially those who have never had a chance. Additionally, many think hell might not even be a real place. What was once airtight theology is now debatable.

The esteemed theologian Michael Green says, "Christians, therefore, should reject the doctrine of conscious unending torment for those who have never heard the gospel just as firmly as they reject universalism."[16] Green believes that those who have never heard the gospel may make it to heaven. "No missionary nerve is cut for him by the possibility that God may save some of the heathen who call upon the name of the Lord as best they can but do not know the name of Jesus— through whom, nevertheless they are reached by God's salvation."[17] Green's theology represents theological rumbling. Humanistic reasoning is shaking the foundations.

When I was young, my mother asked me why I was so concerned about her becoming a Christian. My zeal got the best of me. "Mother,"

I said, "I love you, and I don't want to see you go to hell." This was direct, but the idea of my mother in hell provided strong motivation for my forceful words.

Today the belief in hell among evangelicals is eroding. The danger of hell and the fact it is eternal are important to evangelism. The motive for evangelism is love. If we love others, we do not want to see them suffer. We want them to spend eternity in the blissful presence of God.

Conclusion

I cannot improve on Campus Crusade's definition: "Evangelism is simply sharing Christ in the power of the Holy Spirit and leaving the results to God." The Christian tells others the message of the gospel, seasoned with his own, personal story. But, as Paul put it, "We do not preach ourselves, but Jesus Christ as Lord" (2 Cor. 4:5).

The call to duty will shake some Christians out of their time rut and cause them to make time for outreach, but it will only move a few. The true solution is a vision derived from spiritual vitality, the kind of vision Jesus conveyed to his followers when he said, "Do you not say, 'Four months more and then the harvest'? I tell you, open your eyes and look at the fields! They are ripe for harvest" (John 4:35). Christians must open their eyes to the opportunity of the harvest and the privilege of working in that harvest. We must stop putting off the harvest by arguing that it is just around the corner. There are many high-sounding reasons for delaying full commitment to the harvest, but none of them wash with God. People have the time to reach the world. The question is how they will use it. People will commit when they are captured by the vision of vast, human need and the significant role they can play. They must be transformed from residents to workers. The harvest is now. The only right action is to start working.

.

Appendix 1

J. I. Packer wrote, "Every movement of ideas needs its own literature."[1] The contemporary renewal movement is no exception. I have selected ten writers who are actively pursuing renewal in the church. They are seeking it because they love Christ and his church. Each approaches it from his own personality, life experience, and theological bend.

1. **Richard Lovelace**, professor of church history at Gordon-Conwell Theological Seminary near Boston, Massachusetts, has written what I consider to be the best and most complete work on church renewal available today. In his masterpiece, *Dynamics of Spiritual Life: An Evangelical Theology of Renewal*, Lovelace outlines the history and dynamics of God renewing his people. Lovelace clearly thinks the existing church is worth saving.

"Some critics of the institutional church question whether it is possible for it to achieve disenculturation and would insist on new bottles to hold the new wine. Others who are pastors may theoretically be convinced that the transformation is possible but feel that the inertia and hostility to change present structures in the average congregation make the job so difficult as to be hardly worth the cost." On the other side of the coin, Lovelace asks, "Would starting over with new congregations in new shapes of mission avoid the problem of enculturation? It is a practical certainty that every new gathering of Christians will recapitulate the crisis of disenculturation experienced by the early church as recorded in Acts."[2]

New wineskins relieve the pressure for a short time, but enculturation will eventually surface and take hold. New methods then become traditions and people get attached to them. Form once again begins to dictate function.

Lovelace states his position well in the book's introduction. "The goal toward which many Christians in both Catholic and Protestant communion are striving today is a reformed church always reforming. The Puritans and Pietists rediscovered a truth which is clear in the Augustinian tradition: the precondition of perpetual reformation is the spiritual revitalization of the Church. . . . The great prophets and pioneers of evangelical renewal who looked forward to this ultimate unveiling of the church's grandeur constantly stressed that this goal could only be attained through a strategy of spiritual revitalization combined with doctrinal and structural reformation. I hold this conviction also."[3]

Lovelace clearly supports the investment of time and energy into church renewal. His opinions are highly valuable for their theological precision and historical accuracy.

2. **Howard Snyder** made his mark in 1976 with the publication of *The Problem of Wineskins.* "It is hard to escape the conclusion that today one of the greatest roadblocks to the gospel of Jesus Christ is the institutional church."[4] Snyder proposes a somewhat radical renewal. "For a radical gospel (the biblical kind) we need a radical church (the biblical kind). For the ever-new wine we must continually have new wineskins. . . . First, all church buildings are sold. The money is given to the poor. All congregations of more than two hundred members are divided in two. Store fronts, garages or small halls are rented as needed. Sunday school promotion and most publicity is dropped. Small group Bible studies meeting in private homes take the place of midweek services. Pastors take secular employment and cease to be paid by the church; they become, in effect, trained 'laymen' instead of paid professionals."[5]

Snyder advocates radically changing the existing church but not leaving it behind. His ideas are indeed radical. He also advocates working with the existing church and making major structural change an important means of renewal. He states, "Only those churches which are structured flexibly and biblically will be able to keep up."[6]

It is fair to say Howard Snyder considers church renewal both possible and necessary.

3. In 1984, **George Barna** streaked onto the contemporary church scene with *Vital Signs, Emerging Social Trends and the Future of American Christianity*. As a church futurist Barna seems to be a cross between George Gallup, Alvin Toffler, Lyle Schaller, and Peter Wagner. Without a doubt, he cares a great deal about the cause of Christ.

The title of his 1990 book, *The Frog in the Kettle*, indicates Barna thinks the church is in trouble. He finds that 62 percent of the public think the church is irrelevant and only 19 percent believe salvation defines Christianity.[7] At the book's conclusion, the author lists a number of critical issues facing the church. His list includes winning people to Christ, raising Bible knowledge, establishing community, restoring self-esteem, and focusing on reaching the world.

Barna sees the church locked into the most severe struggle it has faced in centuries. He believes it can be saved, but not without major change. "Clearly, the Christian body cannot hope to have much of an impact if we respond in the same ways we have in the past. These are new challenges, demanding creative, unique responses. The solutions that worked ten or even five years ago will fail in the coming decade."[8]

Like the others, Barna believes the established church can be renewed, but it will require major surgery.

4. **Dallas Willard's** *The Spirit of the Disciplines* ignites the flickering flame of basic Christianity and offers a seminal work for the decade of the 1990s. Willard approaches renewal from an internal vantage point. Rather than dealing with secondary issues of structure and leadership style, he drives a stake through the heart of the matter—the spiritual disciplines.

I heartily agree that the key to effective Christian living is a mastery of the basic disciplines which make one an effective disciple and form the life-support system for the believer. We cannot make disciples unless we master basic Christian disciplines. Willard, a professor at the University of Southern California, has strong opinions about both the disciplines and the church. On the church, he writes, "Generally the church is not doing the job of helping people walk in a deep and meaningful way with Christ."[9] The author points out that the Christian lifestyle is no different than the non-Christian lifestyle, with the same anxieties and depressions.

One of Willard's finest insights is the flip side of Bonhoeffer's cost of discipleship, the "cost of nondiscipleship." Willard says this is much higher than the cost of discipleship.

> Nondiscipleship costs abiding peace, a life penetrated throughout by love, faith that sees everything in the light of God's overriding governance for good, hopefulness that stands firm in the most discouraging of circumstances, power to do what is right and withstand the forces of evil. In short, it costs exactly that abundance of life Jesus said he came to bring (John 10:10). The cross-shaped yoke of Christ is, after all, an instrument of liberation and power to those who live in it with him and learn the meekness and lowliness of heart that brings rest to the soul.[10]

5. **Leith Anderson** represents a new cadre of effective pastors committed to leading churches through renewal. He wrote, "Pain is one of the universal side effects of change."[11] Anderson should know. With patience, strategy, and determination, Anderson led the Wooddale Community Church through the troubled waters of renewal. The strongest apologetic for a point of view is personal example.

In *Dying for Change*, Anderson wrote, "In many ways the Renewing Church is the most promising of the alternatives but the most difficult to sustain. There is constant tension between the old and the new, yet this church accepts the tension as necessary. It would be far easier to fall into old patterns, surrender, or begin from scratch. Instead, the Renewing Church focuses its resources into knowing and fulfilling its purpose."[12]

Anderson embodies a passion for renewal of the existing evangelical church.

6. **Bob Logan**, an international leader in the area of church planting and growth, is committed to church renewal. He started one church and planted seven others from the original during a twelve-year ministry. Recently, he has been helping church planters and existing churches around the world build more effective ministries. Logan ministers internationally on two levels: providing training for pastors starting new churches and offering expertise in church growth principles.

One of his helpful books, *Beyond Church Growth*, now sets a standard for church leaders in search of guidelines. This book gives ten ingredients for a healthy, reproducing church. The ingredients are equally relevant to the existing renewal church. Logan's desire to renew existing churches is on record. "Likewise, pastors who lead existing churches are not adequately equipped for their role by their education. Even lay leaders could benefit from specific training in church growth and ministry."[13]

7. **Frank Tillapaugh** started during the 1970s at Bear Valley Baptist Church in Denver, Colorado, with 100 active members. By 1982, he had built the church to more than 1,000. Tillapaugh has left his mark on the contemporary church through this renewal and with the publication of one of the most important books in the 1980s, *The Church Unleashed.*

Throughout this book, the idea of the church unleashed into the community is contrasted with the concept of the "fortress church." The "fortress church" erects its buildings and starts its programs, but concentrates its energy primarily inside its own walls. On the other hand, the "church unleashed" focuses only part of its energy on what goes on within its church buildings. In the "church unleashed," an individual's ministry may be within a traditional church program, such as Sunday school, or within other ministries such as prison ministry or working with foreign students. As Tillapaugh writes, "The norm is people-oriented."[14]

Like Anderson, Tillapaugh led his church through the treacherous terrain of renewal. *The Church Unleashed* chronicles that exciting but painful journey. Men like Anderson and Tillapaugh have invested much of their lives in the simple proposition that God wants to renew his church.

8. When **Elton Trueblood** passes a country church, he tips his hat. This is his way of honoring the presence of Christ and the labor of God's people who have made Christ's church a reality. Trueblood is one of the great writers, teachers, and churchmen of this century. A generation ago, he rocked the church world with such classics as *The Company of the Committed* and *The Incendiary Fellowship.* His writings have greatly influenced me. Trueblood combines a classical scholar's knowledge and temperament with a churchman's passion and practicality.

Trueblood's commitment to church renewal is legendary. "The church or something like it must be cherished, criticized, nourished and reformed. The church of Jesus Christ, with all its blemishes, its

divisions and its failures, remains our best hope of spiritual vitality.
However poor it is, life without it is worse."[15]

Whether it is the abolition of the laity, the pastor as coach, or the
five steps to a committed church, Elton Trueblood's passion is church
renewal.

9. The renowned scholar **Lyle Schaller** must also be mentioned.
Schaller is a minister to mainline denominations. His books have
greatly broadened his reach. His contributions have touched virtually
all areas of local church life: pastoral search procedure, staff size,
characteristics of different size churches, and various leadership styles
for pastors. His many books and speaking assignments are a hefty testament to his commitment to church renewal.

10. **Ralph Neighbor** is the author of more than twenty-five books.
He has invested a quarter century in church renewal, having pastored
several churches. He now divides his time between Columbia Biblical
Seminary in South Carolina, where he is the director of the Graduate
School of Missions, and Singapore, where he serves as associate senior
pastor of the Faith Community Baptist Church. Neighbor's conclusions are the most challenging of all.

> We must actively abandon the hope that stagnant Churches can be
> renewed by painful restructuring and the tacking on of a cell group.
> . . . According to Jesus, it's not possible to put new wine in old wine-
> skins! The plan for the stagnant Church must begin with the wineskin,
> not the new wine. A Church cannot effectively mix traditional patterns
> of Church life with cell group patterns. There must be a deliberate tran-
> sition. After devoting nearly a quarter of a century to the attempt to
> help renew the churches, I am a total skeptic that it can be done. The
> only hope for old wineskins is to pour out the wine they contain into
> new ones and throw the leaky things away.[16]

Neighbor's arguments are powerful, and his cell-based model is
extremely inviting. In fact, I would encourage all church planters to
pursue the cell-based church as a most effective model for the 1990s
and beyond.

However, Neighbor's skepticism concerning renewal of the traditional church is disconcerting. I do not believe we have permission to
leave the traditional church behind. New wine in old wineskins was a

metaphor employed by Christ to explain why his followers did not need to fast (Matt. 9:17). I do not believe we have exegetical permission to cast an application over the centuries and dismiss conventional Christianity as passé. If new wine is the gospel and old wine Judaism, we have more than structural change at issue. The transition was from law to grace, from old covenant to new, from temple sacrifice to eternal atonement, from Israel to the church. I would need new hermeneutical wineskins to hold the new, exegetical wine required for such a leap. Back then, the new wine was the gospel; it is still the same Gospel. It would be wrong to draw more than a principle from this teaching, and that principle is that new structures are, at best, difficult to make work in old structures.

Another faulty assumption is that we must look at the church as a single wineskin. A local congregation consists of many smaller wineskins. There are also many new wineskins that can be placed into the larger, older wineskins. There is no biblical injunction requiring a complete renewal of every structure. Significant renewal can take place by using existing structures as the vehicles for change. Many churches have successfully done just this.

A third assumption in Neighbor's thinking is that all structural change with pain is bad. True, renewal without pain is a fantasy, but some pain can be both bearable and productive. Theologically and practically, churches can view pain and change as good and, in the long run, necessary for survival.

My fourth disagreement is that Christ has not granted us permission to leave behind the existing, traditional church. "I will build my church," promised Christ (Matt. 16:18). He has given no indication he has stopped working in the stagnant churches. Faithful stewards do not have to like these captives of enculturation, but that does not grant them permission to leave. While many practical arguments can be made for choosing church planting over church renewal, church planting is a form of church renewal. If we are in search of a biblical basis for leaving stagnant churches, we come up empty.

I am sure that many agree with Neighbor's position that the evangelical church is not redeemable, but I am equally as certain that the majority of church leaders, along with the other nine writers mentioned here, disagree. Like myself, most of us feel called to continue the attempts toward renewal.

Appendix 2

A Historical Renewal Model

Church historian Richard Lovelace has developed a model for renewal. Lovelace's model is most complete, built on the twin towers of theology and history. He first presents a renewal model for Israel.

Old Testament Cyclical Model

1. Appearance of a new generation
2. Popular apostasy and enculturation
3. National affliction
4. Popular repentance and agonized prayer
5. The raising up of new leadership

New Testament Continuous Model

I. Preconditions of Renewal: Preparation for the Gospel
   A. Awareness of the holiness of God: his justice; his love
   B. Awareness of the depth of sin: in your own life; in the community
II. Primary Elements of Renewal: Depth Presentation of the Gospel
   A. Justification: you are accepted
   B. Sanctification: you are free from bondage
   C. The indwelling Spirit: you are not alone
   D. Authority in spiritual conflict: you have authority
III. Secondary Elements of Renewal: Outworking of the Gospel in the Church's Life

A. Mission: following Christ into the world and presenting the gospel—in proclamation, in social demonstration

B. Prayer: expressing dependence on the power of his Spirit—individually, corporately

C. Community: being in union with his body—in microcommunities, in macrocommunities

D. Disenculturation: being freed from cultural binds—destructive, protective

E. Theological integration: having the mind of Christ—toward revealed truth, toward your culture.[1]

Before anything else, renewal is an encounter with God. Its precondition is an internal encounter with God; his holiness and our sinfulness contrasted with his Spirit. This is followed by the Holy Spirit's delivery of the "salvation package." Justification, sanctification, possession of the Holy Spirit, and power in battle are the Christian's arsenal. The secondary elements of renewal are too often considered primary. Mission must be built on this spiritual power pack to make progress possible.

I believe Lovelace has correctly distilled the necessary elements for renewal. I believe as well that renewal champions of history have in one way or another tapped into these principles. They have done it by means of the parachurch, and they have worked within existing structures as well. Lovelace issues a warning against throwing out existing structures. "There is a principle of the conservation of structures in the precedent they set. And there are many practical reasons why this principle needs to be followed today. Lines of communication along which renewal can travel can easily be dismantled in any wholesale creation of new structures."[2] In other words, don't destroy your network that will support your renewal efforts, you need it for the flow of information. "The local congregation is like a whaling vessel. It is too large and unwieldy in itself to catch whales, so it must carry smaller vessels aboard for this purpose. But the smaller sailboats are ill-advised to strike out on their own apart from the mother ship. They can catch a few whales but they cannot process them. The smaller boats can easily be destroyed by storms."[3]

Notes

Introduction

1. Howard Snyder, *The Problem of Wineskins* (Downers Grove, Ill.: IVP, 1976), 22.
2. Ibid., 187.
3. Bob Gilliam, Church Effectiveness Survey, 1992.
4. George Barna and William P. McKay, *Vital Signs: Emerging Social Trends and the Future of American Christianity* (Westchester, Ill.: Crossway Books, 1984), 141.
5. Ibid.
6. *Christianity Today,* December 1991.
7. James Hunter, *Evangelicalism, The Coming Generation* (Chicago: University of Chicago Press, 1987), 204–9.
8. Ralph Neighbor, *Where Do We Go from Here?* (Houston: Touch Publications, 1990), 81.
9. James Newby, *The Best of Trueblood: An Anthology* (Nashville: Impact Books, 1979), 26.

Part 1

1. Barna and McKay, *Vital Signs.*
2. Neighbor, *Where Do We Go from Here?,* 14.
3. Gallup Organization, Leadership Network (Denver, 1991).
4. Gilliam, Church Effectiveness Survey.
5. Richard Lovelace, *Renewal as a Way of Life* (Downers Grove, Ill.: IVP, 1985), 136.
6. Ibid., 165.
7. Andrew Murray, *With Christ in the School of Prayer* (Grand Rapids: Zondervan, 1983), 17.
8. Ibid., 23.
9. Gilliam, Church Effectiveness Survey.

Part 2

1. *New Oxford Dictionary*, 6th ed. (New York: Oxford University Press, 1986), 426.
2. Peter Drucker, "Way of Thinking," notes developed by Bob Buford. Used by permission.
3. C. Peter Wagner, Wagner's Observation of Clergy, lecture on "Church Growth Eyes." Used by permission.
4. Bill Hull, *The Disciple-Making Pastor* (Old Tappan, N.J.: Fleming H. Revell, 1987), 190–210.
5. Bill Hull, *The Disciple-Making Church* (Old Tappan, N.J.: Fleming H. Revell, 1990), 32–49.

Part 3

1. James A. Belasco, *Empowering Change in Your Organization* (New York: Crown Publishers, 1990), 2.
2. Stephen Covey, *Seven Habits of Highly Effective People* (New York: Simon and Schuster, 1989), 101.
3. Kennon Callahan, *Effective Church Leadership* (San Francisco: Harper & Row, 1990), 39–58.
4. Bill Hull, *Jesus Christ, Disciple-Maker* (Old Tappan, N.J.: Fleming H. Revell, 1990).
5. Callahan, *Effective Church Leadership*, 50.
6. Warren Bennis, *The Strategies for Taking Charge* (San Francisco: Harper & Row, 1985), 150.
7. Bob Singleton, personal letter to Bob Gilliam, September 9, 1991. Used by permission.
8. Hull, *Jesus Christ, Disciple-Maker*, 65–82.
9. See Bill Hull, *The Disciple-Making Pastor*, Section IV "Making It Work in the Local Church," and *The Disciple-Making Church*, 187–202, 221–50, Appendix by Randall Knutson.

Part 4

1. Hull, *The Disciple-Making Pastor*, 190.
2. Haddon Robinson, *Mastering Contemporary Preaching* (Portland, Oreg.: Multnomah Press, 1989), 57.
3. Calvin Miller, *Spirit, Word, Story* (Waco: Word Books, 1989), 66.
4. Ibid., 190.

Part 5

1. Peter Drucker, lecture at Leadership Network, September 1991.

2. William Easum, *How to Reach Baby Boomers* (Nashville: Abingdon Press, 1991), 58.

3. Sidney E. Mead, *The Ministry in Historical Perspective* (New York: Harper, 1956), 212.

4. Lyle Schaller, *Getting Things Done* (Nashville: Abingdon Press, 1986), 171.

5. Ibid., 173.

6. Kennon Callahan, *Twelve Keys to an Effective Church* (San Francisco: Harper & Row, 1983), 55.

7. Ibid., 57.

8. Ibid., 55.

9. Doug Anderson, "Restructuring the Local Church," at EFCA National Conference, 1987.

10. Jim Peterson, *Church without Walls* (Colorado Springs: Navpress, 1992).

Part 6

1. Scott Peck, *The Different Drum* (New York: Simon and Schuster, 1987), 55.

2. Bob Gilliam, Infrastructure Lecture Notes, The Vision 2000 Training Network, Evangelical Free Church of America, 1–3.

3. Ibid.

4. Ibid., 4.

5. Philipp Spener, *Pia Desideria* (Philadelphia: Fortress Press, 1964), 43.

6. Richard Lovelace, *Dynamics of Spiritual Life: An Evangelical Theology of Renewal* (Downers Grove, Ill.: IVP, 1979), 166.

7. Ibid., 167.

8. Ibid., 193.

9. Don Whitney, *The Disciplines for the Christian Life* (Colorado Springs: Navpress, 1992), 62.

10. Ibid., 15.

Part 7

1. *Christianity Today*, June 24, 1991, 47.

2. Bob Gilliam, Church Development Survey, Denver Seminary.

3. James F. Engel, "Who's Really Doing Evangelism?" *Christianity Today* (December 16, 1991), 35–37.

4. C. H. Spurgeon, *Metropolitan Tabernacle Pulpit* (Pasadena, Tex.: Pilgrim Publications, 1970), vol. 15, 237.

5. John Robinson, *American Demographics,* July 1990, 33–35.

6. George Barna, *Discipleship Journal*, Issue 49, 40.

7. James Speer, Faculty Forum at Trinity Evangelical Divinity School, January 1992.

8. George Hunter III, "Can the West Be Won?" (Christianity Today Institute, December 1991), 44.

9. George Hunter III, *How to Reach Secular People* (Nashville: Abingdon Press, 1992), 36.

10. Hunter, "Can the West Be Won?", 45.

11. Ibid., 43.

12. "The State of Evangelism," *Christianity Today* (December 16, 1992), 35–39.

13. Bob Gilliam and Sharon Johnson, *National Evangelism Survey,* Evangelical Free Church, Church Ministries Department, 1991.

14. Ibid.

15. Allen Tunberg, *The Destiny of Those Who Are Uninformed about Christ: An Identification of Contemporary Views with Reference to the Doctrinal Standards of the Evangelical Free Church of America* (Deerfield, Ill.: Nelson, June 1992).

16. Michael Green, *Evangelism Through the Local Church* (Nashville: Nelson, 1992), 73.

17. Ibid., 78.

Appendix 1

1. J. I. Packer, *A Quest for Godliness* (Wheaton: Crossway Books, 1990), 58.

2. Lovelace, *Dynamics of Spiritual Life*, 208.

3. Ibid., 13, 16.

4. Snyder, *The Problem of Wineskins,* 22.

5. Ibid., 23–24.

6. Ibid., 187.

7. George Barna, *The Frog in the Kettle* (Glendale, Calif.: Regal Books, 1991), 118.

8. Ibid., 223.

9. Dallas Willard, *The Spirit of the Disciplines* (New York: Harper & Row, 1988), 234.

10. Ibid., 263.

11. Leith Anderson, *Dying for Change* (Minneapolis: Bethany House Publishers, 1990), 117.

12. Ibid., 147.

13. Robert Logan, *Beyond Church Growth* (Old Tappan, N.J.: Fleming H. Revell, 1989), 18.

14. Frank Tillapaugh, *The Church Unleashed* (Glendale, Calif.: Regal Books, 1980), 8.

15. James Newby, *The Best of Trueblood,* 26.

16. Neighbor, *Where Do We Go from Here?,* 36.

Appendix 2

1. Lovelace, *Dynamics of Spiritual Life,* 75.

2. Ibid., 209.

3. Ibid., 210.

Bill Hull is the president of T-Net International, a worldwide training network that provides the inspiration, structure, and accountability necessary to help church leaders keep their commitments to God and to experience what they said yes to when they agreed to lead the church. He is a former pastor and former director of Mission USA for the Evangelical Free Church of America.